GUESTCRAFT

FRONT OF HOUSE OPERATIONS

Ann Thunhurst, *Colchester Institute*

Series Editor: Roy Hayter, Hotel and Catering Training Company

MACMILLAN

First published 1990

Published by
MACMILLAN EDUCATION LTD
Houndmills, Basingstoke, Hampshire RG21 2XS
and London
Companies and representatives
throughout the world

Printed in Great Britain by
Scotprint Ltd, Musselburgh

British Library Cataloguing in Publication Data
Thunhurst, Ann
Guestcraft
1. Great Britain. Hotel industries. Receptionists. Duties
I. Title II. Series
647.94
ISBN 0–333–46339–0

CONTENTS

CONTENTS

CONTENTS

ACKNOWLEDGEMENTS

Macmillan Education and the Hotel and Catering Training Company are grateful to Mary James, Beverley Tarquini and Melvyn Teare who helped set up the structure and scope of this book, and to Jennifer Murray who helped edit much of the text.

The publishers would also like to express sincere thanks to the following for their help in supplying photographs and illustrations:

The Alveston Manor (Trusthouse Forte) (unit 23)

Hotel Antoinette, Kingston upon Thames (units 8, 9, 11, 14, 15, 17, 23, 26, 32, 35, 36, 39, 40, 46 and 52)

Baden Powell House, London (The Scout Association) (units 5, 7, 14, 16, 30, 43, 45 and 58)

Bailey's Hotel, London (units 6, 7, 12, 26, 27, 38 and 57)

Beefeater Steak Houses (unit 22)

Catherine Blackie for picture research and photography at Hotel Antoinette, Baden Powell House, Bailey's Hotel, Cromwell Hospital, Flemings Hotel, Gloucester Hotel, Lensbury Club, London Forum Hotel, Princess Louise, Swallow International Hotel, YMCA Hotel

Botley Hill Farm (unit 22)

Brocket Hall (unit 2)

Burford Bridge Hotel, Box Hill (Trusthouse Forte) (unit 4)

Canberra Cruises Ltd (unit 10)

The Castle at Taunton (unit 33)

Caterer & Hotelkeeper (units 10 and 21)

Church Farm Motel, Dereham, Norfolk (unit 20)

Cromwell Hospital, London (units 2, 6, 8, 11, 24 and 53)

Crown Hotel, Harrogate (Trusthouse Forte) (unit 17)

Diners Club International (unit 20)

Flemings Hotel, London (units 43, 49 and 54)

Four Seasons (unit 13)

George Hotel, Colchester (units 12, 19 and 47)

Gloucester Hotel, London (units 1, 12, 16, 20, 22, 25, 29, 35, 38, 45, 47, 48 and 57)

Great Eastern Hotel (Compass Hotels) (units 1 and 21, photographer Picture Link)

Sally and Richard Greenhill Photographers (unit 29)

Heathrow Park Hotel (unit 5, photographer Alex Scaglia, PIMS)

Heyford Manor Hotel, Northampton (unit 13)

Holiday Inn, Mayfair (unit 5)

Horwath and Horwath/Caterer & Hotelkeeper: Horwath-ETB English Hotel Occupancy Survey (unit 21)

The Imperial, Torquay (units 13 and 23)

Kings House Hotel, Glencoe, Argyll (unit 2, photographer Alan Tomson)

Lensbury Club, Teddington (units 3, 5, 6, 10, 18, 25, 41, 43, 44, 50, 51, 53, 54, 55, 57 and 60)

Lloyds Bank (unit 19)

London Forum Hotel (units 10, 22, 33, 40, 43, 46, 50 and 56)

The Marina Post House, Hull (Trusthouse Forte) (unit 23)

NCR (unit 20)

Network/Mike Abrahams (unit 29)

ACKNOWLEDGEMENTS

Park International Hotel, London (unit 49)

Princess Louise, High Holborn, London (unit 19)

Rank Hotels (unit 45)

Regent Palace Hotel, London (Trusthouse Forte) (unit 23)

The Ritz, London (units 18 and 49, photographer Picture Link)

The Royal Lancaster, London (units 13 and 23)

Salisbury House, Diss (unit 18)

Sheraton Hotel, Edinburgh (unit 37, photographer Robin Mathams)

The Sutherland Hotel, Brighton (unit 22)

Swallow Hotels (unit 33)

Swallow International Hotel, London (units 9, 14, 16, 23, 31, 32, 34, 40, 41, 42, 56, 59 and 60)

Tower Thistle Hotel, London (unit 4)

Transmedia (cover photograph)

Trusthouse Forte (units 7 and 13)

University of Surrey Audio Visual Aids Unit (unit 3)

Venice Simplon-Orient-Express (units 7 and 8)

XI Data Systems, Leeds (units 15, 33, 34, 41 and 48)

YMCA Hotel, Surbiton, Surrey (units 9, 13, 14, 26, 30, 39, 42, 48, 51, 52, 53, 54 and 59)

Youth Hostels Association (England and Wales) (unit 3, copyright P Wenham)

The aims of the book

The job of a receptionist requires a lot more than a welcoming smile and a neat appearance. Attention to detail, good administration skills, an ability to recognise opportunities to increase sales and make the most of them – these are every bit as important as good customer care skills.

This book and the accompanying *Guestcraft* video *A Good Reception* aim to help reception and front office staff understand and meet the needs of today's customers. The emphasis is on understanding the reason for doing certain things and providing basic steps that can be applied to all types and size of establishment.

The structure of the book

The book is divided into 60 self-contained units, grouped into eight major subject areas.

The customer—What the customers' needs are and how reception and front office staff can meet them in hotels, other establishments offering overnight accommodation, conference, meeting and exhibition centres, restaurants, theatres and cinemas.

Insight—What providing a good reception requires: the principles. Product knowledge is the basis for meeting customer needs and for meeting business needs by increasing sales.

Equipment and systems—The different items of equipment and various systems in use for reservations, registration, communicating, accounting, obtaining and accepting payment, copying documents, security and producing management information.

The personal touch—The human aspects of presenting a good reception. Communication skills face-to-face, on the telephone, in writing, by fax and telex.

Dealing with—The major section of the book, these 18 units describe the different procedures for dealing with reservations, arrivals, enquiries, complaints, messages, guest bills, departures, taking payment and balancing up.

Legal aspects—How the law affects the provision of accommodation.

Safety and security—Working practices which will help ensure the safety and welfare of customers and staff, and the security of their property, the building and its fittings.

More about—Further details on using keyboards, filing, postal, telephone and financial services.

Each unit has a TO DO, an activity designed to encourage interest, to help the reader apply the information to his or her own experience and so develop a deeper understanding of the subject. Units that will help the reader gain Caterbase modules in reception and front of house are identified.

Whenever you enter any business organisation the chances are that your first point of contact will be at the reception desk / front office. It is therefore important... critical as it sets the scene around which the climate of your visit is built up in advance. therefore.

The first people customers meet when entering an establishment are usually the front office and reception staff. Whether the place is a hotel, hospital, dentist's, hairdresser's, office complex, leisure centre, beauty salon, theatre or restaurant the reputation of the place can stand or fall depending on how customers are treated at this initial stage. This is because first impressions will influence the way customers feel about the establishment as a whole. And it is far more difficult for staff to repair a bad first impression than it is to maintain a good one right from the start of a customer's visit.

Customers will choose one establishment rather than another for a variety of reasons. Some, such as location, are outside the control of reception staff, but others, such as type of atmosphere and service provided, can be adapted to suit the customer. Front of house staff can even influence the decor, facilities and services offered because they are in the best position to discover what customers want and to convey this information to management. A satisfied customer is one who is likely to return, and this is good for business.

A wide range of administrative skills are necessary for any successful receptionist

Why customers visit

Hospitals, dentists, opticians   For health reasons. The receptionist makes appointments and informs customers when it is their turn to be seen.
Beauty salon, sports centre, theatre   Normally for recreational purposes. Appointments are made, queries answered and money is taken.
Conference centre, companies, restaurants   For business or recreational purposes. Some conference centres are used for education and training as well. Customers are shown to the person, section or table they require. In restaurants this task is either done by waiting staff or by someone who is specifically employed for this purpose.
Hotel, apartment block   For accommodation, though hotels may also offer business and leisure facilities.

 *Who are your customers.*

Types of customer

 Customers vary greatly in their requirements. For instance a woman staying at a hotel on business will want different facilities from a couple on holiday with two children under five. It is useful for establishments to group customers into types so that the right facilities and services can be provided.

A receptionist is in a good position to find out what the customers want, and to tell management so that the right services and facilities are provided

Business people   They may be of any nationality using the establishment for business purposes. The visit may be long enough to allow time for recreational activities such as golf, swimming, sauna, squash or massage.
Conference or exhibition customers or exhibitors   They may be either staying at the establishment or using the facilities for only a few hours. They may be visiting individually or as part of a group.
Travellers   They could be sales representatives or tourists. The visit may or may not include overnight accommodation. If customers have a connection to catch, a speedy service could be vital.
Holidaymakers, tourists   They may be British or overseas customers, many of whom will want overnight accommodation which may or may not be pre-booked.
Residents   Some customers live permanently in hotels from choice, or they may be on long-term contracts away from home.

Special offers to encourage customers

Establishments often vary their prices or offer inclusive deals to encourage different types of customers. These terms may include:

Room and breakfast Usually continental breakfast is included in the price, with an additional charge if English breakfast is required.

Half board Room, breakfast and one other main meal.

Full board Room, breakfast, lunch and dinner.

Inclusive terms These may include all daily expenses such as room, all meals, a newspaper and use of sports and other leisure facilities, depending on the establishment.

Discount rates Room prices in particular are offered at discount rates to encourage customers to stay at the establishment, for instance during slack winter months.

Conference rate Special room discounts are offered to encourage delegates to stay, thus enticing businesses to hold conferences at that particular establishment in the first place.

Business, house or corporate rate A discount is given to companies which provide the establishment with a lot of business.

Tour or party rate Lower rates are offered when a booking is made for a large number of people.

Weekend break Lower rates are offered provided the customers meet certain conditions, such as:

* staying at a certain time of year, usually low season
* staying for a minimum length of time
* taking all meals at the establishment.

Theme breaks To encourage additional custom during quiet periods some establishments offer reduced rates for short breaks based around a special activity or interest, for instance a treasure hunt weekend, or Christmas.

✳ FOR INTEREST

Some large apartment complexes known as condominiums have eating and recreational facilities in the same building as the apartments. Though there are relatively few in the UK at present their numbers are expected to increase as demand grows. Center Parcs are a development of the condominium idea.

USEFUL TERMS

European plan Room only.
Continental plan Room and breakfast.
Demi pension or **modified American plan** Half board.
En pension or **American plan** Full board.
Rack rate Full rate business – no discounts are granted.

 TO DO

Before you next visit an establishment where you will be dealt with by a receptionist answer the following questions.

* What kind of establishment are you going to visit – hotel, sports centre, the doctor's, hairdresser's?
* What do you require from the receptionist? Be specific, for instance an appointment first thing in the morning, to wait less than ten minutes, and to be genuinely welcomed.

When you are at the establishment:

* pay special attention to what tasks the receptionist does, for instance arranges appointments, calls the next patient
* observe the receptionist's manner towards customers, for instance polite, brusque, efficient
* study the other customers and try to identify from their

demeanour and what they say whether they are satisfied with the service.

After your visit:

* make a note of the tasks the receptionist did
* make a note on your observations of the other customers
* check against your list of requirements to see which ones the receptionist provided and which he or she failed to meet
* make a note on the aspects of the service you were satisfied with and those you were dissatisfied with
* note two or three aspects of the service you received which could be improved upon, and any which you were particularly pleased with.

Reception duties in premises offering overnight accommodation vary according to the type of establishment, how busy it is, and the needs of the guests. The mornings and early evenings, when most guests check in and out, tend to be the busiest and if the staff are able to work quickly and efficiently, the customers will be pleased with the quality of service.

Sometimes coach-loads of guests will check in at the same time. Where the establishment has shops, conference and leisure facilities, restaurants and bars, for example, there is likely to be a constant stream of people passing the reception desk and requiring attention.

What guests staying overnight want

What guests want will vary according to the type of establishment and the reasons they are staying there. Often the first contact potential guests have with reception staff is over the telephone, when they will ask whether the facilities they require are available, and at what price. A friendly and informative response from the receptionist could mean the difference between a room filled or a room left vacant.

TO DO

From the following list choose and visit at least three establishments in your local area (as different as possible) and find out from brochures and by talking with reception staff what facilities and services each offers to overnight guests/residents. What do these services and facilities tell you about the type of people who use them?

hotels, motels, guesthouses, pubs
hospices
NHS and private hospitals
student halls of residence
condominiums, timeshares
holiday camps, theme parks
ships, ferries, trains, planes
NHS and private welfare homes
caravan parks
company training centres

What overnight guests may want

- room with en suite bathroom
- double, single or twin-bedded room
- bar open until the early hours
- breakfast in bed
- video films
- messages received and passed on
- trained staff available to look after children
- easy access to the room for infirm or wheelchair bound guest
- shoe cleaning, and clothes washing and ironing services or facilities

- room with a view
- orthopaedic bed
- meals available until late
- telephone, radio and television in the room
- clean, tidy room
- early morning call
- choice of continental or English breakfast
- tea and coffee making facilities in room
- choice of newspapers delivered to the room
- family room with cot and extra bed for a child

MASTERCRAFT

See videos *Guestcraft: A Good Reception* and *Customercraft: Keeping the Customers Satisfied*. More details of the organisation structure of hotels and the work of the different departments are given in *Working in the Hotel and Catering Industry*.

Tourist or resort hotels The guests will usually be on holiday and will want to relax and enjoy themselves. Many of these hotels have their own leisure facilities such as swimming pools and tennis courts. Friendly and relaxed service to suit the holiday mood does not mean a lower standard of service.

Motels or motor hotels They are mostly patronised by people on business travelling around the country by car. Some may be lonely and want to chat, others will want to get to their rooms as quickly as possible.

Transient hotels These are near a railway station, airport or sea port. Guests will check in and out at all hours of the day and night and may be on edge. Receptionists need to be skilful at avoiding situations which may cause tension and at checking guests out rapidly.

Residential hotels Catering for permanent residents and often called private hotels. A homely atmosphere may be required here.

Business hotels Used mostly by business people for overnight stays and for conferences and other business meetings. Quick and efficient service with good communication services such as telephones and fax machines may be what the customers require. Most establishments are situated in towns and cities where they are easily accessible.

Educational establishments Many universities and colleges provide

Selling a bedroom is not like selling a bottle of wine which can be kept for the next day. Every night that a bedroom is unsold means loss of potential revenue to the establishment

accommodation for holiday makers and conference delegates during vacations when students do not require the rooms. Bookings are often made for large numbers at one time.

Hospitals and welfare institutions Prisons, homes for the elderly and children's homes provide accommodation for people who do not usually have any choice about whether to stay. Patients and residents are often ill, disabled, elderly or very young, and they may be frightened or apprehensive when they first arrive. Many will be long-stay residents and the institutions will become their only home.

In a small family run hotel, all reception duties may be done by the same person who works behind the bar. This person may even be the proprietor. In such places guests will be expected to park their own cars and might carry their own luggage to their rooms. In a private hospital security staff may be stationed at the reception desk and from time to time help deal with visitors' enquiries

Who does what

Front office manager In overall charge, ensuring that the department runs smoothly and efficiently. Recruits and trains staff. Sets and maintains budgets. Forecasts occupancy levels and analyses past business trends.

Receptionist Registers guests and allocates rooms. Issues key cards or, if used, electronic keys. Processes reservations including correspondence. Deals with general enquiries, messages and complaints. Makes up guest bills and handles cash and credit payments and foreign exchange transactions. Issues and receives cash floats. Sorts and dispenses mail. Liaises with other departments. Sells the facilities of the establishment.

Hall porter Welcomes arriving guests/customers. Provides information and directions. Carries luggage to and from guest rooms (or arranges for porters to do so). Takes messages. Looks after keys for guest rooms. Gives advice on local tourist attractions, transport and so forth. Calls taxis and makes travel and theatre bookings. Distributes guest mail. Helps set up conference rooms.

Night porter Takes over reception duties from 10 p.m. or later to early the next morning. Deals with late arrivals and early departures. Operates the telephone switchboard. Carries out security duties. Provides drinks and light snacks to guests who request them after bar and catering staff have gone off duty. Collects breakfast orders left by guests outside their doors. Distributes newspapers to guest rooms. Helps to set up function rooms.

Telephonist Receives incoming calls directing them to the appropriate person. Takes messages for guests who are not in. Makes early morning wake-up calls. May get international or long distance numbers for guests and management.

Reservations clerk Deals with reservations, advising availability and charges, booking rooms, confirming details by letter, telex or fax.

Cashier Responsible for guest billing and taking payment. Changes foreign currency for guests. Carries out banking procedure.

Cloakroom attendant Accepts customer's coats, umbrellas, briefcases and so forth for safekeeping, issuing a receipt. May be in charge of the cleanliness of the toilets.

Page (In luxury hotels) takes messages to guests, runs errands.

Lift attendant Operates the (non-automatic) lift, escorting customers and staff to the floor of their choice.

Link man Assists and greets people arriving and departing at the hotel entrance by car and taxi.

Security officer Protects the building and its occupants from dangers, theft and undesirable people.

Night auditor Balances the accounts, prepares financial reports, checks cash takings and, in smaller establishments, may carry out night reception and security duties.

Establishments which offer facilities for conferences, meetings and exhibitions as well as the usual eating and sleeping accommodation can boost their profits considerably. Reception and front office staff require good selling skills to match demand for these facilities with availability so that conference rooms are used, and paid for, for the maximum time possible. Delegates will usually have a busy schedule and will require staff to be efficient administrators as well.

Conference centres These are places where conferences, meetings, exhibitions and other events such as advertising launches are held. Centres range in size from a small office, perhaps a converted hotel bedroom, to a huge purpose-built conference centre with numerous facilities including exhibition halls, auditoriums and a range of state-of-the art audio-visual and communications services, such as computers and simultaneous translation from one language to another.

Conferences and meetings Conferences and meetings are usually held for groups of people who either work for the same company or in the same line of business, or who have common pursuits. The organiser normally books the facilities required in advance for instance conference room, microphones, slide projectors, flip charts, video recorders, refreshments, meals and many other extras. The names of delegates are usually given to reception in advance, and will need to be checked as they arrive.

Exhibitions Exhibitions usually last longer than conferences and meetings, and the names and number of visitors who will attend are often unknown because people are not invited individually to attend. An audience is usually attracted through advertising, and so there is no guarantee as to how many will attend. Exhibitions are tiring both to exhibitors and visitors, and so apart from providing the required room and display equipment, enough refreshments and seating must be available to

Conferences, usually for the more budget-conscious, are also held in other forms of accommodation such as halls of residence, university and college buildings, theatres and holiday centres. By opening their doors to conference delegates during vacations and off-peak periods in this way establishments can increase their revenue

If the centre has its own accommodation then the receptionist is responsible for booking that accommodation and billing the individual customers at the end of their stay for items not covered in the conference fee. If overnight accommodation elsewhere is required the receptionist may be asked to recommend an establishment and make the bookings

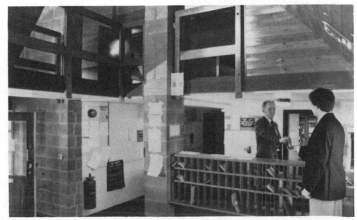

✳ FOR INTEREST

A number of conference centres are being built in country areas where delegates are able to combine business with leisure pursuits such as golf, fishing and walking. Well known examples are the conference venue at Castle Howard in Yorkshire, where the television version of *Brideshead Revisited* was shot, and The Belfry in Warwickshire, home of the Ryder Cup which has two golf courses. Many hotels and conference venues in urban areas also have leisure complexes which conference delegates can use. The Holiday Inn at Heathrow, for example, has eight conference rooms as well as a nine-hole golf course, sauna, solarium, tennis courts and fitness equipment.

accommodate an unknown number of people arriving and leaving at different times. This means that there will be peaks of activity and quiet periods during the day.

Notifying other departments When the arrangements have been confirmed between the conference or exhibition organiser and the conference centre, the receptionist will have to notify the other departments involved. The head chef and restaurant manager should inform kitchen and waiting staff so that the necessary food, drinks and services are provided. Housekeeping staff will have to be on duty to lay out the facilities, organise the bedrooms, and ensure that generally everything is kept clean and tidy during the conference or exhibition.

Reception is the centre of the communications network, and delegates will judge an establishment by the speed and efficiency with which reception staff deal with problems and requests. If these are dealt with satisfactorily, then conference organisers are likely to pay a return visit.

- If ashtrays are overflowing or a cup of coffee has been spilt reception should inform housekeeping so that these can be cleared up.
- If the timing of a function does not go quite to plan, for instance coffee is required ten minutes earlier than arranged, then it is the job of reception to inform the kitchen and the restaurant.
- If equipment breaks down reception should inform maintenance or the hirers so that it can be speedily repaired.

Registration The conference or exhibition organisers may wish delegates to be registered and given promotional material as they arrive. This task may be performed by the receptionist or the organisers may provide their own staff for this purpose. It is usual to have a list of expected delegates who are ticked off on arrival, or to issue identity badges printed with their name and company. If the visitors do not have reservations then these badges will have to be completed as people arrive, which means the receptionist will have to work speedily and under pressure because no one likes to be kept waiting. Sometimes the receptionist will be required only to welcome and register delegates and visitors and deal with enquiries, either at the desk or over the telephone. All administration may be dealt with by other staff.

Occasionally receptionists will be involved in the actual running of the conference, for instance taking notes, running errands and dealing with requests as they arise. Normally the public address system is situated at the front office desk so that the receptionist can put out calls for delegates and visitors when required.

 TO DO

If possible involve four to six of your colleagues in this activity. Split into two groups, one with the task of arranging a short conference (the organisers) for a company represented by the second group (the client company). Separately:

- The client company should prepare as many questions as possible to find out about the facilities available.
- The organisers should prepare a description of the facilities available (this should include advertising material which appeals to the clients and persuades them to confirm the booking), and a checklist of information about the client company which is needed.

The two groups should then meet, acting out their assumed roles. A note should be kept of questions not included on the client's list and of those not included on the organiser's list. Then add any other questions which might be important as a result of discussions. The following headings might help:

General conference requirements   Delegate details
Guest speakers   Social/leisure/entertainment activities
Accommodation requirements:
- meeting rooms
- seating arrangement
- sleeping
- meals
- registration/administration
Arrangements for food, drinks, teas and coffees
Costs and payment details

Restaurants

In most restaurant situations the reception duties are performed by the restaurant manager, head waiter or head waitress, or the waiting staff themselves. These members of staff greet customers as they arrive and show them to their table. Bookings may however be taken by the cashier/ receptionist and in some establishments this person will also escort customers to their table. Bookings are generally taken by phone and get recorded in a diary.

The receptionist needs to have a sound knowledge of menu and wine items and prices. He or she should also be able to tell customers about forthcoming promotions or special themes and create opportunities to sell services and facilities

General procedures

1. Advance reservations should be entered in a book, not on scraps of paper which can easily be lost. The reservations book will need to be referred to by:
   - waiting staff so tables for large parties can be laid up in advance
   - management to plan staffing levels
   - management to analyse sales patterns.
2. Many restaurants will explain to the customer making the booking that there is a time limit for holding tables. This may be 15 minutes for a busy restaurant where each table is used three or four times during the meal service, or 30 minutes if there is only one sitting. Of course if the restaurant is quiet and the guests are particularly late in arriving they will be greeted with considerable (but discreet) relief.
3. In dealing with telephone bookings the response should be warm and interested. Note the customer's name and insert it in the reservations book on the right day, with details about the size of the party and the time of arrival. Bookings from customers who are not well known to the restaurant or not staying in the hotel should be accompanied by whatever information is required to contact the customer in the event of a problem arising. Usually the telephone number and address is taken.
4. Customers without reservations should be seated on a first come, first served basis.

 TO DO

Devise a questionnaire which could be used to find out what customers like and dislike about the facilities and services provided at your workplace. Also provide space for customers to make suggestions which would improve your establishment. Alternatively think of a cinema, restaurant or theatre you visit fairly regularly, and complete your questionnaire from the customer's point of view. These headings may help you:
Decor
Atmosphere
Choice of food/films/shows
Advance booking system
Seating arrangement
Parking facilities
Facilities for families/children
Prices
Quality of the welcome
Standard of efficiency

GUESTCRAFT TIP

Bookings for large parties and bookings made an unusually long time in advance should be confirmed a few days before the customers are due. It is not unknown for customers to change their mind about going to a restaurant yet fail to cancel their booking, or to forget entirely that they have booked a table for a particular occasion. Compensation can be sought when a booking is not honoured (see unit 50), but it is much easier to check the status of bookings in good time, and then be in a position to accept new bookings to fill the restaurant.

Overbooking the restaurant (deliberately or otherwise) is likely to cause disappointment for guests and problems for the establishment. Some popular restaurants do not accept advance bookings, or only accept bookings made on the day concerned. Their customers are prepared to wait for a table if they arrive at a busy time.

Theatres and cinemas

Answering the telephone, dealing with enquiries and taking messages and bookings will occupy a large part of the day for theatre and cinema receptionists. Nearly all theatres and some cinemas take bookings and this requires skill in matching prospective customers with available seats as profitably as possible. Sometimes the box office staff will be dealing with two or three shows, each of which has a different pricing structure for tickets.

Theatre productions are carefully planned in terms of the number of performances and the prices which can be charged for seats to take account of where they are located and the time of the performance. A star name may raise the price of tickets. Complimentary tickets may also have to be issued.

For some shows there is a rush of people just before the performance starts. Everyone wants to buy their tickets quickly and find good seats in time. This is especially true in cinemas where advance bookings are not accepted and seats are not numbered.

At the end of each session sales totals have to be prepared for the theatre or cinema management. Cash takings must be agreed with numbers and categories of tickets sold and then given to management to be banked.

Many theatres and cinemas accept payment by credit card and this makes it much easier for tickets to be sold by telephone. Customers are asked for their credit card details (see unit 46):

- credit card company
- name of card holder
- account number
- expiry date of card

and usually their address and telephone number (in case of a query). If the booking is made sufficiently far in advance the tickets and the customer's copy of the credit card voucher will normally be posted. Otherwise customers will be asked to call for the tickets at the box office before the show starts and produce the credit card to which the cost has been charged as a means of identification.

Booking agents

The theatre or cinema management will negotiate agreements with booking agents whereby a certain number of seats are allocated to the agent to sell. The agent earns a commission on these sales and if the demand for tickets is strong may ask the box office to allocate extra seats. If there are unsold seats available but the box office staff know they can sell the remaining tickets themselves at full price they may refuse the agent's requests. The risk is that long term relations will be damaged in return for a short-term gain.

REMEMBER

People at the theatre, restaurant or cinema are usually out to enjoy themselves. Even though at times you feel you may be the only one working – it is inevitable that reception staff in the entertainment field work unsocial hours – it is important to make sure that the welcome you give customers is sincere. Customers do not want their own enjoyment spoiled by a receptionist who looks tired and fed up. If you genuinely wish them to have a good time at your establishment your smile of welcome will automatically convey this.

The job of receptionist requires a lot more than a welcoming smile and a neat appearance. No amount of friendliness and charm will make up for careless administration. For instance if a customer receives a telephone message and reception staff forget to inform the customer until several hours later, that customer is going to be at the very least annoyed. At worst, if the customer is a business person who has lost business as a result of the delay in receiving the message, then he or she might sue the establishment.

The amount and level of administrative skills required will vary. In a large leisure complex less administration may be performed by the receptionist than in a small hotel because the greater number of guests arriving and departing will take up most of the receptionist's time. In this case the bulk of administrative work will be done by other people such as the cashier and reservations clerk.

Taking reservations

The receptionist receives bookings over the phone, by letter, fax or telex or in person at the desk. It is vital to take reservations correctly. Chaos can result if wrong dates are entered or the number of a credit card or the name of the company responsible for an account is incorrect – not to mention loss of revenue and the establishment's good name. In addition valuable sales and marketing information can be gained when reservations are taken, and if relevant details are carefully recorded establishments can use them to increase business.

The telephone

Answering the telephone is probably the most frequent task performed by the receptionist. A call nearly always contains information which needs to be accurately relayed or recorded by the receptionist.

Where guests' phones do not have a direct dial facility, calls from private rooms will have to go through the hotel switchboard. What the dialler wants is a prompt connection to the right person. If the establishment has a meter system, charges should be recorded on to the customer's bill without delay.

Handling money

Customers' bills are often made up by the receptionist. These should be both accurate and well presented. Few customers want to query a bill and dislike doing so because the information is unreadable or just plain wrong. A lot of revenue can be lost if items are wrongly billed or late charges (those added to the bill after the customer has paid it) are allowed to accumulate. A newspaper, local phone call or breakfast charge left off every fifth bill for instance add up to quite a large sum by the end of the year.

Balancing the money taken is a duty performed by reception staff at the end of the day or shift. The receptionist adds up all the money taken during that day – it may be in sterling, cheques or foreign currency – and makes this amount balance with the figures recorded on the bills and other relevant accounts. If the person receiving payment or charges to the customers' bills has been careless it could take a long time to sort the reason.

Sometimes when customers arrive they will be tired, irritable and unsure of themselves. If so the good receptionist tries that little bit harder to put them at their ease

Whether it is first thing in the morning or last thing at night, whether the receptionist has had a bad day or does not feel very well, every customer deserves a genuine welcome and efficient service. A satisfied customer is one who will return

Forecasts

Preparing statistics which forecast the expected number of customers and revenue for a given period in the future is often the job of reception staff. Other departments will plan their staffing, ordering, special events and activities such as redecorating based on these forecasts. If circumstances change or the forecast does not match reality, then all departments must be notified immediately. Too few or too many staff on duty, under or over stocking of provisions, special events which flop because customer research has been inaccurate can mean extra expense and loss of revenue to the establishment or a lowering of standards of service.

Typing

Typing is another task that is an integral part of the receptionist's duties. Arrival and departure lists, invoices, orders, forecasts, letters, menus and advertising material are a few examples of the documents that require typing and most of these will fall on the desk of the receptionist. For the person or company receiving written communication from a hotel, catering, leisure or tourism establishment the impression will be a good one when:

- the communication looks professional
- the spelling, grammar and punctuation are correct.

However the time spent on these forms of communication must be cost effective, therefore the receptionist needs good typing skills, a good command of written English and an eye for laying out documents attractively. Computers, word processors and electric typewriters which have a small memory can all make the task of typing routine documents and correspondence easier.

Filing

Many documents will be required again and again. For example a letter of enquiry regarding accommodation will form part of the correspondence to be checked before the guest arrives. Usually a number of people require access to files and a logical filing system with easily comprehended headings will help towards the smooth running of the entire establishment.

Dealing with customers

Receptionists are in a prime position to sell the establishment and its facilities and to fulfil the customers' needs.

The warmth of the receptionist's greeting, backed by efficient service, will set the scene for the rest of a customer's visit. One of the most valuable skills a receptionist can possess is that of making customers feel they are valued. No matter how much work the receptionist has piling up, if she or he gives the impression that nothing is too much trouble the customers will not only be satisfied but they will probably recommend the establishment to others. By doing this the receptionist is also selling the establishment.

The ability to work calmly and accurately under great pressure is another skill of the good receptionist. There are times when everything seems to happen at once

When someone is standing at the desk and you are busy, take the trouble to smile and explain you won't be a moment. To the waiting person this response will indicate that he or she has been taken notice of and will be dealt with as soon as you are free. A friendly, prompt response also shows the customer is a welcome and important visitor to the establishment and will be treated with similar courtesy throughout his or her stay

  TO DO

Ask a receptionist you know to describe two incidents where a customer was dissatisfied and the receptionist had to try and put things right. Was the action taken successful? If so, how, and if not, why not?

Dictate.

Selling is about making a profit for your company by satisfying the needs of the customer. Almost everything you do on behalf of your company – perhaps without realising it – is selling. What you are selling are the company's products, services and reputation. A receptionist whose skills in promoting the establishment's conference facilities which had led to a booking, has been selling. Similarly a receptionist who greets customers warmly, is selling because she or he is making a good first impression.

Maximising occupancy *Dictate.*

One of the main tasks of front office staff in hotels, theatres, restaurants, conference centres and leisure centres is to sell space. Space means anything from bedrooms, conference rooms and restaurant tables to squash courts and solariums. A bedroom that remains empty for the night or restaurant table that is not used for two hours is revenue lost. It is money that, unlike selling a sweatshirt or a squash racquet, cannot be made up next day or next week. A single bednight lost can mean anything from ten to hundreds of pounds of lost revenue. A conference hall which remains empty can mean the loss of thousands of pounds and the chance of selling other products and services to numerous delegates. Enormous financial resources are invested in accommodation such as this. Apart from the initial costs of building, rent, rates, electricity, cleaning and repairs all have to be paid for whether the places are being used or not. Maximising occupancy by matching demand for accommodation with availability requires good administrative and selling skills, and is the only way to make a good profit for your company.

The good receptionist knows:
- the full name and address of the establishment
- the postcode, telephone, fax and telex numbers
- how to get to the establishment by all forms of transport
- availability of car parking and the charges
- star rating if a hotel
- number of rooms, their type and cost
- the facilities and services provided and any charge made for their use
- special terms, discounts and packages available
- names of owner and managers
- what chain, group or company the establishment is part of
- what consortium the establishment belongs to
- where other establishments belonging to the same chain or consortium are located and something about their facilities.

Why people buy *Dictate.*

Customers buy for many different reasons.

1 *Price* The price of the establishment may suit the customer's pocket.

2 *Value for money* Customers like to feel that they are receiving the best goods or services within their price range.

3 *Image* Often customers will visit an establishment because it enhances the role in which they see themselves.

4 *Fashion* Because it is the 'in place', the place to be seen, the place to be able to boast about going to.

5 *Competition* There are no other establishments within the area offering the same services and facilities.

6 *Staff attitude* The staff are friendly and welcoming.

7 *Fear* People think they will not find anywhere else to stay or get a meal or drink, for example.

Customers know what they want. It is up to you to find out what that is and provide it

Selling is important to:
YOU: no sales, no custom, no job
YOU: encourages customer to return – job security
YOUR CUSTOMERS: provides them with what they want
YOUR PLACE OF WORK: increased profits
YOUR PLACE OF WORK: development of the company

If the receptionist has an idea why the customer is making an enquiry or visiting the establishment, the appropriate selling action can be taken. Appeal to the correct stimulus can prompt the customer to buy.

Culture The nationality of the customer and what is considered socially acceptable.

Business standing The position the customer holds in working life may affect how he or she expects to be treated by other people and staff.

Social class The person's perception and experience of what is socially acceptable.

Group influences A desire to be seen to be doing the right thing by colleagues, friends and associates.

Selling makes a profit for your company

▶▶▶ TO DO

With a colleague observe six different types of customer in a hotel, catering, leisure or tourism establishment of your choice. Both of you should independently note two or three reasons why each customer is buying the particular service or product.

Compare your observations. If a number of the reasons are similar for different customers discuss why this might be so.

‼ REMEMBER

There is no point in trying to sell something to a customer that he or she does not want. Do not be tempted to push a more expensive item or service because you think it will make a bigger profit for your company. It won't. It will just put the customer off. This does not mean that you should not inform the customer about an item or service if appropriate.

13

When a customer makes an enquiry or a booking, greater satisfaction will be achieved if the person dealing with the enquiry has a good knowledge of the establishment's products and services.

Overnight accommodation The receptionist needs to know the rooms available and their position in the establishment in order to sell them effectively. Some rooms may have different colour schemes and have been more recently refurbished. Some rooms may have a better view. Some rooms will be easier to get to. Some will be quieter.

Regular guests may have a favourite room or part of the building. Details like this should be checked when room allocations are made. A guest who is put for a second time in a room that he or she complained about, is more likely to put the experience down to inefficiency than bad luck.

As a general rule, the better rooms are allocated first. Rooms without a view, or rather noisy because they are above the kitchen or delivery area, should be allocated last.

If customer needs are identified swiftly and an effort is made to fulfil them efficiently, the customer is likely to be impressed with the service

Facilities in rooms The standard of facilities in bedrooms has been steadily improving, even in the least expensive residential establishments. Many student residences have been redecorated and refurnished in order to attract conferences during the vacations. It is rare for a new hotel to be constructed without a toilet and at least a shower for each bedroom. Older buildings are being upgraded to give all rooms private facilities.

Hotel bedrooms are usually provided with a television set, black and white in the least expensive establishments, colour with in-house video channel offering a choice of films in the more luxurious hotels. Many establishments provide free tea and coffee making facilities in every bedroom. Some have a minibar (small drinks cabinet stocked with a selection of miniature bottles of wines, spirits, beers and minerals).

Hairdryers and trouser pressers are becoming more common in guest rooms. Alternatively items which guests may need, such as an iron and ironing board, can be borrowed through reception or housekeeping. Guests can generally arrange for items to be laundered or dry cleaned within a day or so. Usually a selection of soaps, hair shampoo, shoe shines and bath foam is provided. Mini sewing kits, tissues, writing paper, envelopes and postcards are likely to be available. Some hotels provide bathrobes for guest use. Flowers and fruit may be put in superior rooms and complimentary champagne for guests on a special celebration break.

Restaurants and bars Customers may have a choice of restaurants and bars, or the option of room service. In some establishments there are vending machines offering a selection of snacks and drinks at all times.

Reception staff should be able to advise customers on the opening times of restaurants and bars, and describe the menu and some of the dishes available. It is good practice to offer to book a table in the restaurant when a guest checks in. If a special event is taking place, for example a gourmet weekend, or the main restaurant will be closed for a function, guests should be informed when they make a booking.

 REMEMBER

If your establishment is part of a chain or consortium, you should know where sister establishments are located and be able to give details to customers who enquire. If you know where a customer is travelling on to you may be able to recommend a sister establishment and even make a booking.

  TO DO

Make a list of the services and facilities provided at your place of work, or an establishment of your choice and find out as much as you can about them. The following headings may help you:
Prices
Opening times
Special offers
Special events
Facilities in guest rooms
Facilities for children
Access for disabled
Competitive sports events
Menu items
Special foods available

Entertainment Where the establishment provides entertainment the reception staff should know the cost and timings and be able to advise customers efficiently.

Conference, meeting and exhibition facilities Anyone thinking of organising a conference, meeting or exhibition will want to know such details as the size of the different rooms, what sort of event they can accommodate and their capacity when arranged for a particular use.

Theatres and cinemas Many of the enquiries from customers will be over the phone, wanting to know the times of performances, what show or film is on, whether seats are available or there is a bar. These are relatively easy to answer. But what if the customer wants to know what the show or film is about, who the main performers are, and whether it would be suitable for a friend who understands little English? The only way to answer these questions and to sell the product successfully is by seeing the film or show yourself. Most managements are sympathetic to this view. In this way any real enthusiasm from you will be apparent to the customer who may be encouraged as a result to book tickets. Giving a false picture, whether deliberately or through ignorance, will not help you to sell your product. A customer who is disappointed by a show because he or she was led to believe it would be something else may not pay a return visit, whatever the next show. A good knowledge of seating arrangements and ticket prices is also important to ensure that the customers get what they want at a price they can afford. Many theatres now run systems where tickets can be booked for several shows at a time at reduced rates. Being able to inform customers about this could boost ticket sales considerably.

Leisure complexes and sports centres More and more activities and facilities are being provided at leisure and sports centres. Many are keen to encourage the whole family to attend while others are more exclusive and charge high membership fees. The receptionist should know what facilities are available, when and at what cost. What the potential customer can afford is another aspect to consider. A customer able to pay a reduced rate at off-peak hours for a game of squash, say, is better than no customer at all.

A receptionist who knows the product well can immediately give the customer the information which is required

The organisers of conferences and meetings have a wide choice of suitable venues, including the exclusive and novel

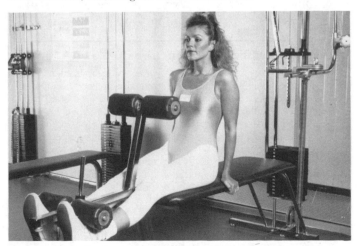

In many cases the decision on a venue will take into account what leisure and entertainment facilities are available in the area

The process of marketing goes hand in hand with selling. The Institute of Marketing defines marketing as being able to anticipate, identify and satisfy customer needs profitably.

Market research will help the establishment find out what type of customers it can attract and what kind of services and facilities should be provided. Once this is determined the company will then set out to create an image which will say a lot about the kind of establishment it is and be easily recognisable to potential customers.

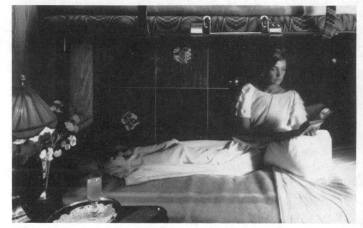

If customers do not want a product or service there is no point in providing it because they will not buy it

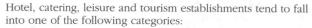

Hotel, catering, leisure and tourism establishments tend to fall into one of the following categories:

- privately owned such as a family run hotel
- company owned such as BUPA hospitals, Sheraton Hotels, Center Parcs
- franchised such as Wimpy (the private owner pays a well-known company for the use of its name and image)
- privately owned but a member of a consortium such as Prestige Hotels
- publicly or state owned such as NHS hospitals and residential homes, local authority swimming pools.

Putting across the right image

As the receptionist is usually the first person visitors will meet, he or she should conform to the image expected. Otherwise visitors feel uncomfortable and out of place.

Some establishments have a company policy on how the telephone should be answered, for instance, 'Good morning' followed by the name of the establishment and receptionist, and then, 'how may I help you?'. Most people like familiarity and will be reassured by this response since it is what they expected. Registration and booking procedures may also be standardised which means the receptionist must be trained to sell facilities in a certain way. Other establishments expect their reception staff to learn by experience as they do the job

In a leisure centre used by families with young children the receptionist may be required to wear a brightly coloured track suit, whereas a receptionist in a hospital may be more soberly dressed and more formal, though still friendly, in approach

Large companies and franchises

Large companies may own a wide variety of establishment with images designed to appeal to many different types of people. In this case the similar establishments are grouped together, given the same name and marketed together. Trusthouse Forte have done this with their Post Houses, Travelodges and Little Chefs which conjure up very different images from each other. When an establishment is franchised or company owned it reaps the benefits of extensive marketing and advertising and a well known image already recognised by the customer. The responsibilities of the receptionist working in an establishment which is part of a group or chain includes recommending the other establishments to the customers. In many cases the receptionist will be able to make reservations in other company or consortium establishments, directly by computer link or telephone, or with a central reservations office.

A good receptionist is aware that he or she is on show and that behaviour, dress and manner all contribute to portraying the right image for the establishment and the company

A customer who feels at ease is less likely to complain and is easier to satisfy than one whose expectations about an establishment are not fulfilled

Advertising and promotional material

The larger companies spend thousands of pounds on advertising and promoting their establishments. Smaller establishments may have to be content with advertising in the classified section of the local paper and word of mouth. Just as the receptionist is part of the image, so advertising and other promotional material should hit the right note. Some ways in which an establishment or company will promote itself are:

- editorial features in newspapers, magazines and other media
- advertisements in the press and other media
- links with airlines, travel agents and tour operators
- guidebooks, for instance the tourist boards, RAC and AA have a grading systems for hotels according to the facilities and prices charged
- central reservation systems
- point-of-sale promotional material (located in the establishment itself) such as logos, tablemats, special events, gift certificates or vouchers, and posters.

Brochures are one of the principal ways of selling an establishment through the printed medium. In addition to the main brochure which describes the various facilities and services available other brochures or leaflets will be used to promote special events and offers. These may range from sponsored charity events to mystery weekends.

Sales letters are a way of bringing details of what is available to the attention of potential customers. Carefully written, well presented and individually addressed, for example to Mrs Hughes, they can make the person receiving them feel the establishment places a high value on satisfying its customers.

Examples of special packages

Budget breakaway   Two nights accommodation at weekend only, with optional third night, full English breakfast, dinner on both nights, packed lunch on one day. Extra charge for single rooms. No charge for children under 14 years of age sharing room.

Nightaway   One night stay only (Friday, Saturday or Sunday), including accommodation, breakfast and dinner.

Conference rate   Minimum ten delegates. Includes all conference facilities, morning coffee, buffet lunch, afternoon tea. Residential option includes dinner and overnight accommodation.

Celebration weekend   Price for two people includes superior room/suite, flowers in room, complimentary bottle of champagne, all meals.

Leisure breaks   Minimum four night stay including weekend, includes use of leisure facilities, accommodation, breakfast and dinner.

▶ ▶ ▶   TO DO

Look at the following conversation between a sales representative, Mr Brown and the receptionist at a company-owned hotel which has other establishments in most of the main towns and cities of Britain. Identify where the receptionist failed to create a sale.

Good morning, Mr Brown.
Good morning. May I have my bill, please.
Certainly, Mr Brown. I won't keep you a moment. Here it is. The account is to go to your company, so would you sign the top copy, please?
Thank you. I have to go to Birmingham now. Have you any idea how long it will take me to get there?
About two hours, I should think. Have a good journey.
Goodbye, Mr Brown.

Now rewrite the conversation so that the receptionist creates a sale for the company.

Almost every contact the receptionist has with the customer should provide an opportunity to sell. This is known as a sales lead. In order to sell successfully the receptionist needs to know:

- about the products and services available
- how to recognise each customer's motive for buying
- how to direct the conversation to create sales leads.

In order to get a fair understanding of why a customer wants to buy, the receptionist needs to listen to the person and ask questions, and then if necessary provide information about the establishment's products, services and facilities.

Because	*so you may need to*
customers may not always ask for what they need	tell them what is available
they may not realise what is available	
products and services may have changed since their last visit	
they may need to be told about what is available	describe what is available
they may have forgotten what is available	suggest or recommend
they may not have made up their minds	
they may be embarrassed to ask	ask them what they would like

But the receptionist may still need to do more to find out exactly what the customer's needs are and what can be sold to meet these needs. Further *watching, thinking, listening, informing, asking* may be required.

Benefits and characteristics

Customers will only buy something which they want or need, in other words something which they will benefit by. Customers who believe, for instance, they are about to buy a bargain or have a good time will consider these to be benefits. If the receptionist tries to sell them something they feel will not benefit them they will probably get annoyed and may never return to the establishment, which means custom lost.

Each benefit has characteristics which provide facts to show customers just how or why they will benefit from a particular product or service, for example:

Benefit	*Characteristic*
You will have the opportunity of a good long sleep, Mrs Duke.	BECAUSE Your room looks on to the gardens, so you will not hear any noise from the main road.
You will be able to exercise regularly during your stay, sir.	BECAUSE We have a fully equipped gym and a sauna to relax in after.

GUESTCRAFT TIP

If your establishment does not provide the services or products required, then recommend a place nearby that does. This will earn goodwill from the customer who may then pay a return visit.

Some hotels keep a set of jump leads, de-icer, damp start and an emergency petrol can in reception for use by guests who have a problem with their car. The more standard range of emergency supplies will include toothpaste and toothbrushes, disposable razors, shaving foam, ladies' tights, elastoplast, aspirin, disposable nappies and cotton wool

Successful selling is often achieved by showing concern for the welfare of the customers. Friendly and polite conversation will often reveal the real thoughts and feelings of customers which will help the receptionist to discover what products or services can be sold to satisfy those needs

Seeing selling in terms of benefits and characteristics is useful because it links the product or service with the customer and his or her needs. It is only too easy to go on about the product itself:

Receptionist 'Our gym boasts the latest German-made body building equipment... tested by Dolly Timpson, you know the chap who's an athlete... it's always very popular with our visitors...'

Customer (thinks) 'What's all this got to do with me? I wish that receptionist would stop going on and on.'

The good receptionist

- Sells the establishment and its products and facilities.
- Greets customers in the manner that will create the right image of the company.
- Matches requests for services and facilities with those available.
- Distributes accurate and up-to-date information to both customers and visitors.

▶ ▶ ▶ TO DO

Make a note of how you would describe the benefits and characteristics of certain products or services to the following customers visiting your workplace or an establishment of your choice. Write them as though you were the receptionist speaking to the actual customers – the benefit followed by the word 'because', followed by the characteristic.

Benefits
- start with the word 'you'
- come before the characteristic
- make sense when linked to the characteristic with the word 'because'.

Characteristics
- use the words 'we' or 'they', not 'our'
- come after the benefit
- describe things.

1. 'We promised to make this our second honeymoon, even though we've got the kids with us.'
2. 'I can never resist a bargain.'
3. 'What a hectic day.'

✱ FOR INTEREST

The accommodation industry is growing fast. Tourism, both local and overseas, is increasing every year, and is one of the largest growth industries in the UK and many countries throughout the world. More and more people have time and money for leisure activities, including holidays. Day trippers are being catered for by the huge development of theme parks and leisure centres, some of which also offer residential accommodation. The private hospital sector is also expanding as more people are insured for private medicine, and offer services on a par with hotels. With the expansion of multi-national companies and the huge growth in general of the business sector, conferences have become regular events for business people, and specialist business hotels have developed to cater for their needs which often include overnight accommodation. The non-business sector is also becoming increasingly specialised, catering for specific groups of customers. For example teenagers spend a high proportion of their income on leisure activities and they are some of the main customers of theme parks. At the other end of the age range people are living longer as healthcare and education improves, with the result that there is an increase in demand for residential homes for the elderly. Pensioners are travelling too and going on low-cost coach and rail holidays in the UK during off peak periods.

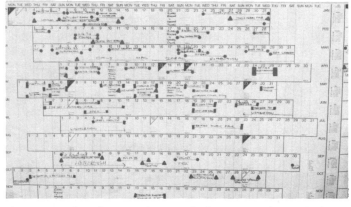

A summary of conferences, shows and other events going on in the area throughout the year is a sales tool as well as a reminder of busy periods. An alert receptionist will pick up clues from booking enquiries about events which should be added to the wall chart. These sales leads can bring in further business for the establishment

There is always just that little bit more the receptionist can sell to the customers. This does not mean being pushy. Provided what is sold is still what the customer wants or needs everybody will benefit – the customer, the establishment and the receptionist.

YOU	YOUR CUSTOMER	YOUR WORKPLACE
You feel good because you have helped to satisfy the customer's needs	Your customer is more satisfied	The company's profits are increased

Add-ons

The additional products or services that the customer might benefit from are called *add-ons*. You should:

Watch for clues about the customer's needs, for instance the guest who has just booked in for a night stretching his arms and rolling his head in discomfort.

Listen for clues about the customer's needs, for instance the customer telling another that travelling makes the muscles seize up.

Think what else the customer might require, for instance a workout in the establishment's fully equipped gym – the add-on.

Up-sell

This is when you sell something more expensive than the customer initially planned. One way of making the customer want the product or service is to compare the benefits of the more expensive product with those of the cheaper one, and so show the customer what he or she would lose by not buying it. For example:

Watch Mr and Mrs Bagthorpe come into the hotel foyer dressed more formally than usual.

Listen 'It's our wedding anniversary.'

Motive Pleasure.

Benefit 'If you are looking for a special evening, Mr and Mrs Bagthorpe, I am sure you would enjoy dining in our roof top restaurant.'

Characteristic 'We provide very personal service, relaxing music and dancing.'

Comparison 'The food in our coffee shop is very good.'

Loss 'But you would miss out on the romantic atmosphere.'

 REMEMBER

Never use a comparison to run down a competitor's product or service.

Down-sell

As well as selling a little bit more to the customer the establishment can also benefit financially in the long run if you sell a little bit less, that is a product or service that is cheaper than the one originally requested. For example:

In a leisure centre
'For a first visit, Mr Atlas, you might find a two hour session a little long. How about booking one hour first to see how it goes?'

At the opticians
'I agree with you, Miss Clavelly, these glasses suit the shape of your face better than the more expensive ones.'

Down-selling is appropriate in these examples because the member of staff is attempting to meet the customer's needs in the best way possible. Knowing when to down-sell is also a matter of watching, listening and questioning to find out exactly what your customer wants. Where the establishment benefits is that the satisfied customer is likely to return, and to tell friends of the quality service received.

Substitute selling

Up-selling and down-selling are both forms of substitute selling. You sell something different from what they originally asked for. There are three situations where substitute selling might be appropriate:

1. When the product or service the customer asks for is not available. 'I'm sorry, madam, but all the grass courts are booked. Perhaps you would like to try one of the hard courts?'
2. When the product or service that the customer requests is not provided by your establishment. 'I'm sorry, Miss Gimble, but there are no coach trips arranged for this afternoon. But I can arrange for you to join the guided walk round the old town.'
3. When you think a different product or service will meet the customers needs better. 'Why not dine in our roof top restaurant, Mr and Mrs Harrison-Prentice?'

> ◆ ◆ ◆ **TO DO**
>
> Think about an occasion when you have, perhaps without realising it, been involved in substitute selling. Write down the steps you took in making the substitute sale and compare them with the following:
>
> 1. *Watch, listen, question* to find out the customers' motives and needs. Then if substitute selling is appropriate:
> 2. *Explain* that what they request is unavailable or not provided or that they might prefer something else.
> 3. *Select* the alternative product or service.
> 4. *Describe* the product or service using benefit and characteristic comparisons (see unit 9).
> 5. *Reinforce* the customers' decision to buy the alternative because they may want reassurance. For instance, 'I'm sure you'll enjoy the old town, Miss Gimble. The guide is an expert on the architecture and social history of the area.'
>
> Make a note of any you need to practise.

A floor plan is a useful reminder of the location of particular rooms. In many establishments it is the policy to allocate the best rooms first. In quiet periods guests might be given a superior room to the one they booked, at no extra cost. This creates a good impression and it is quite possible that on return visits the customer will request and be happy to pay for the superior accommodation

EQUIPMENT AND SYSTEMS

In order to match what customers want with what is available, the basic requirements are: a record of reservations relating to each day and a means of knowing quickly if a booking can be taken for a particular day or period (see also units 31 to 34).

Reservations chart

The conventional or traditional chart (also known as the room or bed chart) is drawn up or pre-printed with one line for each room and one box for each day of the period covered by the chart.

- Write the entry in pencil so that it can be easily changed.
- Draw a continuous line from the middle of the square representing the day of arrival to the middle of the square representing the day of departure, with an arrow at each end.
- Print the name of the guest just above or just below the line, with any other appropriate text such as VIP.
- Try to ensure the guest will be in the same room throughout his or her stay. This may mean re-organising other, shorter bookings.
- If a specific room has been requested, make a note to this effect so the booking is not moved to another room later.

Most charts cover a month, but some establishments work on a weekly or fortnightly basis. A particular room is allocated to the guest at the time a reservation is made so bookings may have to be moved around the chart to maximise occupancy

Density chart

If the average length of stay is quite short it is easier to use a density chart. The chart consists of a row of boxes for each type of room for each day. The number of boxes corresponds to the number of rooms available.

Say a booking is taken for a single room for three days. The next free box in the single room column for each of the three days is cancelled out or blocked in. This is done in pencil so cancellations can be erased.

Room numbers are allocated just before guests arrive (see unit 35).

A variation on this system (used in large hotels before computerisation) employs two scales. Bookings are first marked off on the section of the chart where one box corresponds to one room. When ten rooms have been sold one box is marked off on the less detailed chart. In this way a hotel with 300 single rooms will have one very large chart with 300 boxes. A second smaller chart will have just 30 boxes, showing the booking situation at a glance.

Another variation is the inventory chart. This uses figures instead of empty boxes. So if there are 30 twins there will be a row of numbers 30, 29, 28 and so forth down to minus figures if an over-booking allowance is included. When the first booking is taken for a twin the 30 is crossed off, showing at once that there are 29 twins still available.

Stop–go chart

This chart typically takes the form of a year planner. A symbol is used for each room type, for instance a silver star for single rooms. When a certain type of room is sold out on a particular day, the appropriate symbol is stuck on the chart. Receptionists can see room availability at a glance.

Diary or room book

This usually has one page for each day. It can be used if there is insufficient space on the reservations chart to record the time of arrival, for example or method of payment. In small establishments, say a guesthouse with six rooms, a diary can replace the need for a reservations chart. Room numbers are written down one side of each page and the guest's name is recorded against the appropriate room for each night that the guest intends to stay.

Alternatively the reservations are written in the diary on the appropriate page as they are received. This has the disadvantage that they are not in room order. The diary can be ruled up into a series of columns:

- room
- name
- departure date
- terms
- time of arrival
- reservation method
- date reservation made
- confirmation received
- special requests.

When a reservation is cancelled or changed to a different date a line is put through the original details and a note of explanation added.

Rack systems

Rack systems such as Whitney (a patented name) were very popular before the widespread use of computers. A typical system consists of a series of metal racks which hold small cards. When a reservation is made a card is completed and placed in the advance reservation rack for the day of arrival, in alphabetical order. At the top of the card in the area that is always visible are recorded the important details:

- name of guest
- date of arrival
- date of departure
- number of people
- room tariff/terms

with other information in the lower part of the card such as address and telephone number. A particular colour card can be reserved for each type of room, for example blue for singles, white for twins. Where there is a different part of the rack for each type of room, colour coding can be used to indicate other details such as pink for VIP guests, yellow for a travel agent booking.

If the booking is changed to a different date, the card (often called a shannon) is moved as appropriate and the details on the card amended.

Computer systems

Many establishments now use computer systems, with all the advantages they bring of speed, reliability and versatility (see units 14, 18 and 56).

As soon as the reservation details are entered the computer will check room availability and if the requirements can be met, record the booking in its memory. Reservation details can be called up in any convenient format, for example in alphabetic or numeric order, by room type or date of arrival.

▶ ▶ ▶ TO DO

Take a large sheet of paper, ideally A3 size (420 x 297 mm) and ruled or divided into squares (for example graph paper) and draw it up as a reservations chart.

1. At the top of the paper (and this should be along the longest side) label it with a month and year of your choice, then draw up and label the vertical columns you will need for:
   - room number
   - room type: use abbreviations such as T/B (twin-bedded), D/B (double-bedded), S/B (single-bedded), or the simpler T, D and S
   - each day of the month (1, 2, 3, 4, 5 and so on to 28 or 29, 30 or 31 depending on the month and year you have chosen).
2. Down the side of the paper draw up and label horizontal columns for an 11 bedroom hotel: 8 twin-bedded, 2 double-bedded, 1 single. You will need one horizontal column per room. Make up your own mind for each room number whether it is a twin, double or single.
3. Pencil in the following reservations, assuming you receive them in the order listed below:
   Wahab: twin, arriving 6th, departing 12th
   Brunel: single, arriving 2nd, departing 3rd
   Stevenson: double, arriving 14th, departing 20th
   Mackinson: double, arriving 19th, departing 21st
   Schmidt: twin, arriving 1st, departing 7th
   Boulez: single, arriving 9th, departing 11th
   Cohen: 3 twins, arriving 7th, departing 15th
   Midland Tours: 3 twins, 2 doubles and 1 single, arriving 5th, departing 8th
   Midlothian Engineers Ltd: 4 twins and 1 double: arriving 8th, departing 16th
   Cardiff Rovers: 8 twins, arriving 16th, departing 18th
   Watson: 1 twin, arriving 7th, departing 8th
   Movenpick: 3 twins, arriving 15th, departing 16th
   Mulcher: 1 single, arriving 15th, departing 27th
   Sherlock: 1 twin, arriving 13th, departing 16th.
4. If Mrs James phones to reserve a single room, arriving 8th, departing 10th, decide what you can offer her and assuming she accepts, pencil in the reservation.

Reservation forms

Reservation forms or booking slips are specially designed for taking the details of reservations made by telephone or in person.

- They are easily recognisable and therefore less likely to be lost than a scrap of paper.
- They encourage a logical progression of questions as the receptionist gets all the necessary details.
- The receptionist is encouraged to use the form as a checklist. She or he is less likely to forget either to give information to the guest or to ask for important details.

Essential details

from person making booking

Name of person for whom accommodation is required	Mr/Mrs/Miss/Ms or title
Address	Telephone number(s)
Date of arrival	Date of departure
Number of nights stay	Number of persons requiring accommodation
Type of accommodation required	
Price to be charged	Estimated time of arrival
Method of payment	Whether confirmation required
Any special requirements	Name of person making booking (if different), address and telephone number

of staff who handle booking

Signature/initials of person taking booking	Date booking taken
How long provisional booking will be held for	

Useful details from person making booking

How establishment heard about:

- advertisement
- recommendation
- previous customer
- brochure

Follow-up action checklist

- reservation on computer/chart
- brochure sent

The customer's enquiry can provide valuable sales leads. Say a reference to attending an art exhibition is the first news of an event that will bring many visitors to the area. Approached carefully the organisers provide details of all exhibitors. The manager immediately sends a personalised letter describing the hotel's facilities and a copy of the brochure. This is followed up by a telephone call and the result is a full hotel at a time when it is usually less than a quarter full

Confirming reservations

It is the usual practice to confirm all reservations in writing. This establishes the existence of a contract more clearly (see unit 50 and units 31 to 34) and gives both parties an opportunity to check that the details of the booking are correct. It also gives the establishment a further chance to sell its services, and to indicate the value placed on its customers. For example:

- the confirmation letter can briefly describe the new restaurant and invite the customer to book a table on arrival
- a brochure and information leaflets on local attractions or details of a special event can be sent with the confirmation
- a handwritten letter from the proprietor of a guesthouse suggests very personal service and a small establishment
- a typed letter on good quality letterhead can reinforce the customer's expectations of luxury, style and personal attention
- a telex or fax message gives immediate confirmation, demonstrating that the establishment can respond to customer requirements to communicate rapidly
- a pre-printed confirmation slip with the details completed by hand or printed by a computer will give a travel agent or the regular hotel user the impression of a business-like approach with streamlined administrative systems that help keep costs (and therefore prices) competitive.

Word processors and computer-based reservations systems make the task of confirming reservations straightforward (see unit 14). Standard paragraphs can be merged with personalised information quickly and with some systems the details entered into the reservation system will transfer automatically to the confirmation letter or slip.

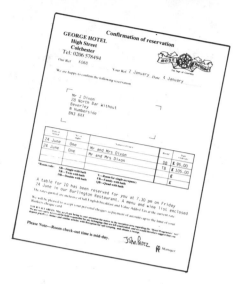

Standard letters and pre-printed reservation slips provide a convenient method of communication and are useful for reminding customers of certain conditions such as the check-out time. But used thoughtlessly they indicate impersonal service to the customer. If they make no reference to particular requests, contain inaccuracies, are poorly laid out or misspell the customer's name they will give a poor impression of the establishment and its staff

 TO DO

Take a large sheet of paper, preferably A3 size (see units 12 and 17) and ruled up into a grid of small squares. Divide the longest edge of the paper into seven equal vertical columns, one for each day of the week and starting on the left with Sunday. Make it up into a density reservations chart for a 50 bedroom hotel for the week of April 8 to 14. Organise the chart so that particular types of room are grouped together under a sub-heading:

- twins (of which they are 35)
- doubles (of which they are 5)
- singles (of which they are 5)
- superior twins (of which they are 5).

Allow for a small over-booking margin: 3 rooms for the twins, 1 room for each of the other type of room. So if you have chosen small circles to represent each room available use a small square to represent the over-booking allowance. You will therefore need to draw:

- 35 circles and 3 squares for each day of the week under the heading *Twins (35)*
- 5 circles and 1 square for each day of the week under each of the other headings: *Doubles (5)*, *Singles (5)* and *Superior twins (5)*.

Ask a colleague to give you a series of bookings, including some cancellations and amendments. Here are a few to start you off.

1. Kingston Rotary Club: 5 twins and 1 double Friday 13th.
2. Saga Holidays: 7 twins and 1 single arriving Sunday 8th, departing Saturday 14th.
3. Mr Symthe: 1 single Wednesday 11th.
4. Mrs Jahal: 1 single arriving Thursday 12th, departing Monday 16th.
5. Mr Haral: 1 superior twin arriving 10th, departing 13th.
6. Mr Symthe cancels.

Registration records

Some small hotels and guesthouses use a hard covered book rather like a visitors book to register their guests. This system is convenient when there are unlikely to be several guests wishing to register at the same time, and the guests do not mind everyone who has access to the book knowing their full name and address and when they have stayed in the establishment concerned.

Individual registration cards or forms are more convenient for busy establishments and give the guests greater privacy. They allow sufficient space for the extra details that overseas visitors must complete. (See unit 50.)

Essential details for every guest seeking accommodation	Useful details
Full name	Method of payment
Nationality	Home address and telephone number
Date of arrival	Company address and telephone number
	Date of departure
	Signature of guest
	Car registration number
	Purpose of visit
	Occupation
	Has person stayed before: Yes/No
and	
if an overseas visitor	*completed by receptionist*
Passport number and place of issue	Number of guests
Address at next destination and date of departure	Room number
	Room charge
	Source of booking
	Date of arrival and departure (if not completed by guest)

No legal requirement to register

Persons under the age of 16 years

Foreign diplomats, their families and staff

Some registration cards have a tear-off section which when completed forms the guest's key card (above) or the card for the room board (left). The card above was part completed by the receptionist before Mr Per checked in

Key cards

Key cards serve two purposes.

Information They are a useful means of reminding the guest about meal times, latest departure time, methods of payment, safe deposit facilities, the room tariff and so forth. When attractively designed and printed they also form effective promotional material, advertising the services and facilities of the establishment and of the parent company.

Security They provide a means of identification for the guests, which can be produced when keys are requested or bills presented for signature (see unit 53). If the guest keys do not carry a room number (another security precaution) the key card also acts as a reminder to the guest of his or her room number.

The details should include:

- room number
- date of departure
- name of guest or guests

optional

- signature of the guest
- room tariff.
- date of arrival

Some companies issue special key cards to guests on weekend breaks or similar arrangements which include meals normally paid for as an extra. This makes it easy for staff to identify which guests do not have to be presented with a bill. It may not even be necessary for them to be asked to sign the bill provided their room number has been established at the time the table reservation was made or the meal order taken.

The Royal Lancaster

Please show this card e
time you collect your k

VALUABLES:
We draw attention to the notice displayed in the front hall regarding the liabilities of the Hotel Proprietors. The Hotel Proprietors cannot hold themselves responsible for any valuable that may be left unattended. Jewellery, money and valuables should be deposited with Reception for safe keeping and a receipt obtained.

*LEISURE FACILITIES:
There is a passive games area in the Gates Bar. Our sister hotel the Hotel Nelson has a Sauna, and arrangements can be made for guests to use this if desired.
Local leisure facilities — Reception will be pleased to furnish you with further information.

ICE AND DRINKS:
When the bar area is not open drinks are available all day from the Duty Manager and at night from the Night Porter who has a drinks fridge.

Breakaways Available Throughout the Year

 TO DO

Design a registration form which could be used by a medium-sized hotel. The form should be easy to complete and as well as obtaining the details required by law it should ask for any information which you feel will be useful for marketing purposes.

Make some photocopies of your form and ask six or seven friends to have a go at completing it. Check how they got on.

- Did they find it easy to use?
- Was there sufficient space for the details they were asked to give?
- How did they react to the additional questions you had included for marketing purposes?

If necessary revise your form to take account of these reactions. Then show it to two or three experienced hotel receptionists, if possible working in different establishments. What are their views? Discuss how the form could be adapted to take account of specific procedures and circumstances, for example:

- by including a tear-off section for reception staff to record details required for the room board
- by including a reminder that valuables should be left at

reception for safekeeping otherwise responsibility cannot be accepted for them

- by designing the form so that it can be re-used each time a particular guest stays in the hotel (with the dates of arrival and departure and other such details recorded on the reverse of the form)
- by the use of different languages so that overseas guests with a poor understanding of English can complete the form without help.

Discuss with your friends and with the receptionists how the process of registration might be made easier. For example:

- What details can be completed in advance on behalf of the guest? And if forms are completed in advance how can they be found quickly by the person dealing with the registration?
- How can a disabled guest who has difficulty completing the form be helped?
- How can guests be reminded that the registration details should be given for each person staying?

The switchboard

Receptionists will be required to operate the telephone switchboard if the workplace does not employ a special operator. There are various types of switchboard, the most common being the PABX (private automatic branch exchange). It comes in several different models with trade names such as Herald and Monarch, but they all work on the same principle. The operator answers incoming calls and any internal calls (from within the establishment) which are routed directly to the switchboard.

With a PABX switchboard staff and customers within the establishment do not have to go through the switchboard when they want to talk to each other. They can also dial outside numbers direct, but sometimes long distance calls have to be made by the switchboard operator. Modern switchboards can be programmed to allow all types of call to be made from certain extensions only.

On PMBX (private manual branch exchange) equipment the operator has to connect all calls manually using a system of switches or plugs and cords.

Public address equipment

The public address (PA) system is usually operated by the same person as the switchboard. It is used for contacting customers for instance when a telephone call is received and the operator is unsure of the person's whereabouts. Basically it is a microphone system which, as its name implies, is carried through speakers to the public areas such as the foyer, restaurant, bar, lift and lavatories. Some traditional hotels still use a page boy, normally the most junior member of the hall porter's team, whose job is to walk through the public areas to look for the guest, if necessary calling out the name. This can give the impression of a more personal service.

Telex

The telex machine is used for receiving and sending written communications via the telephone line. It combines the speed of a phone call with the reassurance of the written word (see units 29 and 32). The message is typed out on a keyboard similar to that of a typewriter or computer and written copies are printed out at either end. Telex equipment is usually sited in the same area that

The reception desk and front office are the nerve centre of communications both within the establishment and to the outside world. Information in the form of messages, letters, fax, telephone calls, verbal communications, telex, computers is constantly transmitted to and from customers, members of staff in other departments, and companies the establishment has to deal with

In establishments where reception staff have to handle a wide range of enquiries from visitors wishing to use the leisure facilities, for example, as well as incoming telephone calls, the public address system will be located under the reception counter

advance reservations are dealt with. Telexes can be transmitted all over the world where there is the equipment to receive them. Hotel guests and especially conference delegates are often given access to the telex for which they pay a fee.

Fax

The full name for the fax machine is facsimile telegraphy (see unit 29). It is similar to the telex machine in that it uses the telephone line to transmit and receive almost instant communications throughout the world. But it does not require typing and can reproduce pictures. It works in a similar way to a photocopier, except that the copies are produced at the receiving terminal, possibly thousands of miles away. It is usually found near the telex machine and can be operated by the same person. Although the fax machine is a fairly recent development, it is already in use in a great number of hotel, catering, leisure and tourism establishments. It is easier to operate than a telex machine and much less expensive to install. The cost of sending a fax is the same as the cost of making a telephone call to the same destination. It depends on the distance involved, duration of call and when the call is made (see unit 59).

Computers

Computers can process information far more quickly than people can. They are particularly useful where:
- there is a large amount of information to be processed – as in working out occupancy percentages for each type of room over the last month, or calculating the value of stocks held
- rapid communications are required – for example between housekeeping and front office so rooms can be let immediately they have been cleaned and checked, or between the reservations office and other hotels (in the same country and abroad) belonging to the same company where guests might be encouraged to make bookings
- speed and accuracy are very important – as in dealing with reservations, guest billing, and accounting (see unit 18)
- the information processed is repetitive – for example confirming reservations, or sending sales letters to a large number of potential customers, or logging all telephone calls to keep records of the number called, the time and duration of the call, the cost of the call and who made the call
- information kept for one purpose is used for another purpose, perhaps with some modification – for example presenting reservation details for a particular day in the form of an arrival list, or transferring charges for guest telephone calls automatically to the appropriate bills
- managing complicated technology – controlling heating and lighting to make more efficient use of energy, for example, or controlling room locks and producing electronic keys or key cards programmed to operate the lock to a a particular guest room for the duration of the guest's stay.

There have been immense advances in the technology of communications equipment and systems in recent years. Some establishments, especially the larger ones where a lot of information needs to be transmitted, are fully equipped with the latest machinery. Others find that the telephone and a typewriter are sufficient

How computers work and their uses are covered in the information technology units of *Working in the Hotel and Catering Industry*.

▶ ▶ ▶ TO DO

Find an establishment that is not computerised. Make a list of the areas in the front office that may be computerised and indicate the order in which you feel they should be computerised. Your decisions should take account of the advantages (and disadvantages) of computerisation for both customers and staff, and other implications such as training, cost savings and capital investment. Note your thoughts on these.

The bigger the establishment the more important it is to have a good system for communicating information about the people due to arrive or depart, who is staying at any particular time, what functions are taking place, which people should be treated as VIPs and so forth.

In some cases a simple list is all that is required. For example to remind reception staff of who is due to arrive on a particular day the information contained in the booking system and on the correspondence file can be summarised in a list of:

- the name of each person due to arrive
- type of room booked
- number of people in party
- number of room (if one has been allocated in advance)
- the length of stay and/or departure date.

If this list is arranged in alphabetical order then the receptionist can deal efficiently with an arrival:

'Good evening, may I help you?'

'I have a reservation.'

'What is your name please, madam?'

'Wahab.'

'Yes, here we are, Mrs Wahab. We have reserved a single room with bath for you for two nights. I'll get the key, in the meantime would you kindly complete this form to register. You should please put in the details of your passport.'

Information on departures can be produced separately so the cashiers, for example, know what bills to prepare.

Combined lists of arrivals, departures and guests already in the hotel will give the various departments the information they need to do their work efficiently:

- housekeeping staff – what rooms have to be cleaned and prepared
- porters – what rooms luggage has to go to or be collected from
- telephonists – what rooms calls for guests can be transferred to and if there is no answer to know whether it is because the guest may have departed or has probably not yet arrived
- bar and restaurant staff – confirmation of who might be signing for drinks and meals
- all staff – details of special requests such as wine in the room, warning about important guests, early arrivals or late check-outs.

The way in which the list is organised will depend on its purpose. For example, housekeeping staff will require a list by room number, telephonists a list in alphabetical order.

Room status list

Reception staff will usually produce from their records a

Listings of arrivals, residents and so forth cannot usually make clear from the name alone the number of persons in each room, for example if Mr Jones is sharing a twin bedded room with his son the list could simply indicate 'Mr D Jones'. This is the reason for the separate column showing the number of sleepers, guests or residents in the particular room. In the event of an emergency the list of guests in house (or combined arrivals/departures/residents list) will provide a means of checking that everyone is out of danger, so it is vital that the details are accurate

daily list of every room and its status:

- occupied by a guest staying over or member of staff, when the name(s) of the occupant(s) will be given and the number of occupants
- to be vacated (a departure)
- vacated but still to be serviced
- vacant and ready for use
- taken out of service and the reason (for example redecorating).

Housekeeping staff can check the actual status of the room against the list and report any discrepancies, for example a room let to one person obviously occupied by two, or a room which was let but has not been used at all.

Alternatively housekeeping staff produce their own room status list, for example when the head housekeeper inspects all the rooms. The details which will be checked by reception staff later include:

- let (occupied) and the number of sleepers (this may not be clear)
- vacant to be serviced
- vacant and ready for re-letting
- out of service.

Room board

The room board has a slot or card holder for each room in the establishment. The details of each guest are recorded on a card and inserted into the appropriate holder. An empty slot indicates that the room is vacant. Alternatively a system of coloured cards can be used, for example red to indicate the room is being cleaned, yellow to indicate the room is available for letting and green to indicate the room is occupied.

The Whitney room board operates on a similar principle. Coloured plastic slides can be used to indicate the status of the room, so when a guest has arrived the receptionist moves the slide to yellow. Coloured lights are another way of showing room availability. When the system is linked to the house-keeper's office, he or she can change the light on the reception panel from red to green as soon as the room is ready.

The guest details can be recorded on a number of identical cards at the same time by using NCR (no carbon required) paper. One card remains in reception, another goes to the telephonist, another to the porter's office and so forth.

Bedroom book and bed sheet

The bedroom (or bed) book is used in some smaller hotels to give a permanent record of the status of each room. For every day of the year there is a list of all the room numbers with space opposite to indicate the names of the room's occupants, or notes such as 'redecoration'. If the room entry is blank it is, or was, vacant.

A diary with one or two pages per day can be ruled up to make a bedroom book and in this way can be combined with the reservation record system (see unit 11). A photocopied list avoids the need to write out each room number once for every day of the year, but it is less durable than a hardbound diary and there is a risk that individual sheets could be mislaid.

When the information on room status is on a sheet of paper a further advantage is that it can be photocopied and distributed to everyone who needs to know what rooms are occupied, will be occupied or are due to be vacated. This can be indicated by the use of symbols, notes or by organising the details in three columns: arrivals, staying, departures.

Function lists

If meetings, dinners, conferences or other functions are held in the establishment regularly, it is useful to circulate a summary of the events taking place:

	For example
date	3 April
who the hosts/organisers are	Colonel and Mrs Tait
what the event is	luncheon party
where it is being held	Highlands Suite
time	12 for 12.30 p.m.
numbers of guests expected	25
special instructions	guests may ask to see equestrian centre

The list will usually be circulated to all staff involved in the organisation of the event and to front of house staff so that they can direct guests to the appropriate room and deal with any related enquiries. Whether the list is produced daily, weekly, or monthly will depend on the amount of function business done by the establishment.

 TO DO

Here are some of the special requests that might be found on an arrivals list and which would clearly be the responsibility of the housekeeping department to organise or supply: foam pillows, extra bed, cot for infant child, bed board.

Consider what other special requests the guests of a luxury hotel might make and draw up a list, indicating against each item what department(s) or member(s) of staff would be responsible for providing it.

If for some reason details of special requests were not made on the arrivals list but on a form devoted to this purpose what do you think the form should look like? Have a go at designing your own request form. When you are reasonably happy that it will suit its purpose, photocopy it and ask a few colleagues to have a go at completing it. Encourage them to think of their own special requests. Have they thought of any you should add to your own checklist? Does your form ensure that the necessary details are obtained and made available to the appropriate staff?

Communicating with people on the move
Certain members of staff have to move around the building much of their working day. Managers, housekeepers, maintenance engineers, porters, security officers and other staff whom it may be necessary to contact quickly can be issued with a message calling machine or 'bleeper'. This is activated from a central control point, usually at the telephone switchboard, when it will make a bleeping noise. This alerts the wearer who can contact the control point from the nearest telephone. Some message machines have a small screen on which is displayed the telephone number of the person who has to be contacted or another short message. Other models send out a pulse strong enough for the person to feel (provided the machine is kept on the person, say in a jacket pocket). This is more discreet than a bleeping signal.

Noticeboards are an accepted way of communicating information and bringing messages and mail to the attention of residents and visitors in certain circumstances. In a home for the elderly, for example, the residents are usually well known to each other and are unlikely to steal or tamper with someone else's mail. In many commercial establishments the risks of this happening are too great and so noticeboards are more useful for leaving messages to conference delegates, for example. Even then the message may be kept deliberately uninformative to an outsider, or the person asked to contact reception or the conference office, when all the necessary details can be passed on

Other lists

VIPs If the hotel has a lot of VIPs a special list of their names and status (Mayor, for example) will save staff having to look through a long arrivals and departures list for the remark 'VIP'.

CIPs An alternative name for the VIP list, preferred in establishments where management and staff think in terms of *Commercially Important Persons*.

Early arrivals If the pattern of business is very varied, for example at an airport hotel, it will help housekeeping and other staff if they get a special report with the details of those who will be checking in early.

Early morning calls This records what time guests wish to be given an alarm call in the morning.

Newspapers A list of what newspaper(s) each guest wishes to have in the morning.

This takes the guesswork out of the daily newsagent's order and reduces the risk of guests being disappointed because the hotel has run out of copies of their favourite newspaper.

Guest history cards

Some establishments keep a personal record of each guest. This is quite time consuming if the cards have to be written by hand and filed, but computers can store large amounts of this sort of information, produce it easily and quickly and many of the details can be added automatically from other records, for example dates of stay, method of payment. When a booking is made the computer can search the records and remind the reception staff that the guest complained on his last visit, or she had to be booked out as the hotel was overbooked.

Pigeon holes behind the reception or porter's desk are a more secure way of keeping messages and mail until they can be given to the person they are intended for. If the room key is kept in the same place the member of staff responsible for handing over the key can see immediately when there is something else to give to the guest. Ideally the pigeon holes should be out of sight of customers and casual passers-by, or if this is not possible the room number identifying each pigeon hole and key should be small. It is then much more difficult for a dishonest person to see which of the building's occupants are out leaving their possessions relatively unprotected (see unit 53)

Complaints book

A special book or form is often used for recording details of complaints made by customers. This makes it easy for the management to keep an eye on the level of customer satisfaction. It can also provide a means of checking that complaints are acted upon (the book includes a separate column for follow-up action). If a complaint is received after the customer has left the establishment then the details can be checked with the complaints book – it is not unknown for customers to turn a minor lapse in service or a small problem into a major catastrophe.

Black list

This highly confidential list is kept as a reminder to front office staff of the people who are not welcome at the establishment, for example because they have not paid the bill on a previous occasion, or because they have been abusive to other guests and staff. From a distance it should look like one of the many other lists or documents receptionists have to refer to regularly (see unit 37).

The list may also include names circulated by the police, for instance people who are suspected of terrorist activities or believed to make a practice of defrauding hotels.

If the guest history records are held on computer and automatically checked when an enquiry is made or a registration processed it is likely that the black list will also be computerised.

 FOR INTEREST

Registration details and other records such as enquiries, complaints, bookings and guest comment slips can be very valuable in market research. They can indicate significant trends, help build up knowledge of customer expectations and so improve the level of customer satisfaction.

 GUESTCRAFT TIP

In busy reception areas several members of staff may require particular documents or to use staplers, calculators or other small items of equipment. If care is taken to leave such resources in their usual place then the work of everyone will be made easier.

The internal telephone system allows reception to transmit and receive information quickly from other departments. Verbal requests, say a room needs an extra bed at the last minute, are best followed up in writing to avoid any misunderstanding and to make sure the appropriate adjustments are made to the guest's bill

 TO DO

Ask a colleague to write a letter of complaint to you as manager of a hotel, catering, tourism or leisure establishment. Consider what action you would take, list each step and draft a reply. Check with your supervisor or tutor that you have covered all the main points and also what action you would take if your colleague visited your establishment again. For example would it be appropriate to offer the person a free bottle of wine (if you have chosen a restaurant situation)?

In front office operations much of the equipment and many of the systems are similar to those used in the offices of local authorities, government departments, banks and commercial firms of all types and size. Indeed receptionists often carry out quite general secretarial duties and need to be familiar with paper and envelope sizes, for example, and know how to display menus and price lists attractively.

Stationery

Most establishments will use a range of stationery.

Printed letterhead This will be pre-printed with the name and address of the establishment, the telephone number, fax and telex number if any, and usually a logo or other design device unique to the establishment or company. The quality of the paper will tend to reflect the image the establishment wishes to convey. Luxury hotels, for example will use very high quality paper and the printing may be in more than one colour, possibly on coloured paper. Some letterhead is embossed. This more expensive process builds up the printed characters so they are raised above the surface of the paper giving it a more exclusive feel. Letterhead is often kept in two sizes so that short letters do not look lost on a large sheet of paper. Lightweight versions will be available if there is a regular need to airmail letters overseas.

Envelopes Where an establishment uses special paper for its letterhead – a particular quality or a certain colour – there are usually special envelopes. These will complement the stationery sometimes to the extent of carrying the logo and even the name and address details. A smaller size of envelope is best for the smaller letterhead and lightweight envelopes for airmail (these should use the standard international airmail design and colours). Less expensive plain envelopes (often made with brown paper) are useful for routine correspondence with suppliers – confirmation of orders, payment of bills and so forth. Window envelopes have a section on the front which is covered with transparent paper. This allows the address on the letter to show through and saves having to type the address a second time.

Carbon paper This is the traditional method of copying letters, memos and other typed documents at the time they are prepared. A sheet of carbon paper is placed between the top copy and a second sheet of paper, with the copying surface of the carbon facing the second sheet. Carbon paper can be used to make as many as four copies at the same time, but a photocopier is easier to use for multiple copies especially if corrections have been made during the typing (see unit 22).

Copying paper Lightweight paper is generally used to make carbon copies of documents. It is less expensive than letterhead or even plain bond paper and less bulky. This means files are more manageable and additional carbon copies will be more legible (particularly if the typewriter can be adjusted to strike the paper with more force).

Menus help sell the products of the restaurant and bars and contribute to special celebrations such as a birthday party. They should not only be accurate and without mistakes, but look nice. A popular format is to centre each line – straightforward with a word processor or good electric typewriter that will automatically count the number of characters and spaces between the words. Where there are two or three dishes for a particular course they should be grouped together and extra space left between each course or a symbol such as an asterisk used

Menu

TOM & BELLA LINES
70TH BIRTHDAY DINNER
27TH FEBRUARY 1990

SELECTION OF HIGH CLASS MEATS
* * *
SOLE BELL BONNE FEMME
* * *
THE CROWN OF THE YEARS
WITH FULL REGALIA
* * *
SELECTION OF VEGETABLES
* * *
GATEAU SURPRISE
LE SOIXANTE-DIX ANNIVERSAIRE

FOR INTEREST

Paper sizes have evolved over many years. For commercial use the standard sizes are identified with the letter A and a number. A1 is the largest size, A2 is half the size of A1, A3 is half the size of A2 and so forth. The A4 to A7 range covers most office use:

width   *length*

A4   210 mm x 297 mm   used for reports, most letters and memos
A5   148 mm x 210 mm   used for shorter letters and memos
A6   148 mm x 105 mm   used for postcards
A7   74 mm x 105 mm   used for compliment slips

Letterhead and general-purpose paper is usually ordered by the *ream* (500 sheets). The weight of the paper is measured in grams per square metre, abbreviated to *gsm*. Paper for general use is usually 80 gsm, good quality letterhead will be printed on a heavier paper, for instance 100 gsm.

A5 letterhead is sometimes preferred with the address on the longer side (210 mm). This style is called *landscape* – as opposed to *portrait* when the address is on the shorter side (148 mm). Postcards work equally well in portrait form and many people prefer landscape compliment slips.

Automatic sorting machinery used by the Post Office will accept envelopes of certain sizes: not less than 90 mm x 140 mm and not more than 120 x 235 mm. Envelopes which fall outside this range have to be handled manually and so their progress through the mail is slower. Reply-paid envelopes and postcards (pre-printed with the addressee details, see unit 58) must be of a certain size to conform with the licence, and special Post Office services such as bulk mail discounts are only available for POP-sized documents.

Envelopes come in standard sizes denoted by the letter C and a number. The most common sizes are:

- C5 which takes an A4 sheet folded in half or an unfolded sheet of A5
- C6 (also known as DL) which takes an A4 sheet folded twice to one-third its original length or an A5 sheet folded in half.

If the opening of the envelope is on the longer side it is known as a *banker's envelope*. *Pocket envelopes* have the opening on the shorter side. The cheaper envelopes have to be dampened to activate the glue and form a seal. *Self sealing envelopes* merely have to be closed (bringing two glued areas into contact so they bond together) or a strip of paper removed to expose a glued area which will then form a bond when the envelope is closed. *Trap envelopes* have no glued surface. The flap is tucked in which means the contents of the envelope can be examined, for example by customs or by a post office if the items are being sent as printed paper (less expensive than normal mail in some instances). *Non-trap envelopes* have a more sophisticated closing device so there is no risk of the contents of the envelope falling out or other, smaller envelopes slipping through the opening.

 GUESTCRAFT TIP

When using a window envelope make sure that all the address details will be visible throughout the handling process. Type the address in the right place and fold the letter correctly so all the address can be seen through the window and the paper will not slip around at a later stage in the envelope. Some letterhead has guide marks to show where the address should start and for each fold – for example a small dot that the recipient of the letter will not notice.

▶ ▶ ▶ **TO DO**

Have a go at designing your own letterhead for a hotel, catering, leisure or tourism establishment of your choice. Before starting make a checklist of the points which you would have to tell the printer or designer responsible for producing the finished job. Include such details as the image you want to convey, quality, colour and weight of paper, size(s) of letterhead, whether it should be portrait or landscape.

 REMEMBER

Menus are one of the principal ways of selling food. They also have to give certain details (sometimes easily overlooked by the busy receptionist who has to type them), for instance:

- the day and date and possibly the year
- the meal (breakfast, lunch, dinner)
- the price of the meal (for set price or table d'hôte menus)
- the price of each dish (for à la carte menus)
- any restriction on choice (for example either soup or hors d'oeuvres).

There are three main methods for front office accounting:

- the tabular ledger, a manual system based on a large book ruled into a number of columns. It is a slow method of keeping guests' accounts. Errors are easy to make and time consuming to trace. The scope for analysing charges by department is limited by the number of columns available
- the hotel billing machine, a machine with similar capabilities to a good cash till. Like cash tills the range varies from basic models many years old to sophisticated modern machines which are more like computers
- the computer plus appropriate software. Some hotels use a basic accounting program, or there are various front office/hotel accounting packages.

Tabular ledger

The columns of a tabular ledger enable the various charges guests are likely to incur – accommodation, meals, drinks in the bar, room service and so forth – to be kept separate and analysed by department.

If a more detailed analysis of charges is required, there will be separate columns for each bar, for example, for lunch and for dinner. If guests are likely to incur a number of charges from the same department two or more lines will be allocated to each room to prevent the figures getting over-crowded. A separate sheet is used for each day or more than one if the hotel has that many rooms.

Most tabular ledgers have the list of guest rooms and names running vertically down the left-hand column. The various departments to which charges are allocated run horizontally across the top of the page. Sometimes it is more convenient to have the room numbers running across the top of the page.

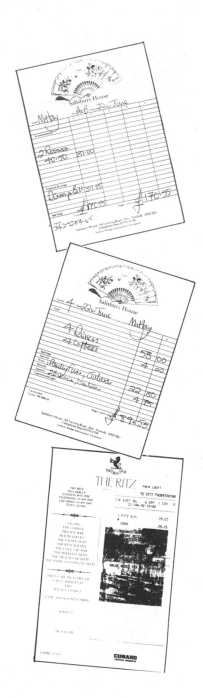

Billing machine

Hotel billing machines have some of the capabilities of a computer and look and work like the cash tills used in shops and supermarkets. They are programmed to record different categories of products, facilities and services by pressing the appropriate key. The receptionist may also be required to key in his or her own identification number. Typical features include:

- automatic storage of the balance on a large number of different guest bills, so that when a further charge has to be added or the bill total is requested the previous balance does not have to be re-entered
- running totals kept of total charges by department or category
- record printed on paper tape of all transactions
- vouchers overprinted with the details of the particular transaction thus providing a means of checking the voucher has been processed and what bill the item was charged to
- balances on all account categories printed on request, say at the end of the shift
- balances on all account categories cleared to zero on request, say at the end of the business day.

Computer-based systems

Computers provide a means of integrating many of the front office systems – reservations, room status, information processing, billing – with the overall accounting and management function (see unit 56). For example:

- a bill is opened automatically when the computer is told the guest has arrived
- charges are posted to department accounts and to the guest bill at the same time and all the details are held in the computer's memory (unlike the billing machine which usually only keeps a running total)
- slave terminals, for example in the bar, communicate with the central computer to add charges directly to guest bills
- credit control listings can be produced of bills over a certain limit
- all the details making up a guest's bill, or charged to a department account, can be displayed on the monitor and printed out on request
- the operator is guided through the appropriate sequence by instructions and prompts displayed on the monitor.

▶▶▶ TO DO

Obtain some A3 accounting paper (pre-ruled into columns) which you can use for setting up the tabular ledger for the Guestcraft Hotel on 11 November. Working from left to right, label the vertical columns as follows (the numbers below are for your guidance only – there is no need to number the columns):

1. Room number	2. Name	3. Sleepers (number)
4. Accommodation	5. Restaurant	6. Bar
7. Telephone	8. Room service	9. Paid outs
10. Sundry	11. Daily total	12. Brought forward
13. Total	14. Cash	15. Allowances
16. Ledger	17. Carried forward	

1. Enter the following guest details: Room 1 Mr Dewar, Room 2 (vacant), Room 3 Mr/s Maloney, Room 4 (off), Room 5 Mr/s Jameison, Rooms 6 and 7 (vacant), Room 8 Mrs Patel, Room 9 Sir Arnold, Room 10 Miss Arnold.

2. Enter the number of sleepers and the accommodation charge. Assume this is £70 for a twin room (that is rooms 3 and 5), and £40 for a single room (the other guests).

3. Vouchers are given to you for the following:

   Sir Arnold, dinner £28.65   room 10, lunch £8.75
   Mr and Mrs Maloney, dinner £35.00 rooms 9/10, laundry £4.80
   room 3, room service £10.74   paid out room 9, £12.00
   Mr Dewar, telephone calls £3.75   room 1, bar £3.75
   Sir Arnold, telephone call £1.28   Mrs Patel, magazines £2.25
   Sir Arnold, bar £12.50   room 5, laundry £3.25

4. Enter these various charges on the tab, then work out and enter the daily total for each guest.

5. There is a brought forward amount for room 1 of £65.65 and for room 8 of £82.50. Enter these in the brought forward column and enter the total amount now owed by each guest in the next column.

6. Sir Arnold has settled his bill and Miss Arnold's bill in cash. Mr and Mrs Jameison have paid by credit card (also enter in cash column). Mr Dewar has signed his bill and it will be forwarded to his company for payment (enter in the ledger column, see unit 46). The Maloneys are staying on (enter in the carried forward column).

7. Mrs Patel has complained about the meal she had from room service and the manager agrees to cancel the charge (enter in the allowance column). She pays her bill by cash.

8. Total each column and enter the amounts at the foot of the column.

9. Check the ledger entries balance (see units 47 and 48):
   - the total of columns 4 to 10 should agree with the total of column 11
   - the total of columns 11 and 12 should agree with the total of column 13
   - the total of columns 14 to 17 should agree with the total of column 13.

From time to time front office staff, especially those working in small establishments, will encounter documents and systems that relate to the business generally.

Petty cash vouchers If a small sum is kept in cash for minor purchases, paying taxi fares for staff who have finished duty late and so forth, each payment must be supported by a petty cash voucher (preferably with the receipt attached to it). The amount of petty cash is fixed (in the same way as a cash float, see unit 48). When it is due for replenishment any remaining cash plus the value of the petty cash vouchers should agree with what was originally issued. Each voucher should:

- be dated
- give the value and sufficient details to explain the expenditure
- be signed by the person who made the expenditure/claimed the money
- be countersigned by a person with authority to approve the expenditure.

A petty cash book is used to help analyse what petty cash has been spent and generally record the movement of money. It is usually divided into a number of columns with such headings as 'Stamps', 'Staff transport' and 'Newspapers'.

Bank paying-in slip This is used to summarise monies deposited into the establishment's bank account. Most banks issue their customers with a personalised paying in book pre-printed with the customer's name, account number and the bank's own code. (See units 48 and 60.)

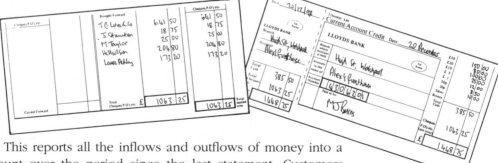

Bank statement This reports all the inflows and outflows of money into a particular bank account over the period since the last statement. Customers who have a large number of transactions may request daily statements, but a week or month is more usual.

The statement will give the date and nature of each transaction, for example counter deposit, bank charges, cheque payment (with the cheque number), standing order and direct debit (with appropriate reference details). Some banks print details of the payee on statements.

After each transaction or group of transactions the balance in the account is indicated – followed by the symbol 'Dr' if the account is overdrawn and therefore in debit.

Each transaction on the statement has to be reconciled with the other financial records: do cash receipts agree with the records of what was deposited in the bank, do payments agree with records of cheques issued and so forth? It is not unusual for the balance in the bank to be higher or lower than the establishment's records indicate. For example, if a cheque to a supplier has not yet been cleared by the banks involved the balance will be higher. On the other hand if a cheque from an account customer has not yet been cleared the balance will be lower.

Requisitions These support requests for items from stationery and food stores, the cellar and other internal departments that store and control purchases in advance of their use. The requisition form should:
- be dated
- indicate the department the order is required for
- give quantities and a sufficiently detailed description of what is required
- bear the signature or initials of the person ordering and any supervisor or manager who has to authorise the request.

Purchase orders These give the details of items ordered from external suppliers. If a sales representative has taken the order, or the order has been made on the telephone written confirmation can help both parties.

Pro forma invoice A pro forma invoice is used when the goods have to be paid for in advance. It is similar in appearance to a normal invoice but if a decision is taken not to proceed with the order the pro forma lapses. By comparison a normal invoice is a demand to pay for goods already received. It cannot be ignored.

Other supplier's documents A *delivery note* should accompany any delivery from an external supplier. It gives the person responsible for receiving the order the means of checking quantities and other details such as the quality of the goods. Discrepancies should be recorded on both the establishment and the supplier's copy of the delivery note so that the invoice will be correct.

The supplier's *invoice* will detail the goods or services which the establishment has received and agreed to pay for. It shows the price of the different items supplied, any discount, the VAT amount and the total to be paid. Efficient suppliers quote the order reference details on the invoice.

A *credit note* will be issued by the supplier if goods already invoiced have been returned or an adjustment is agreed which reduces what the establishment is due to pay. If the invoiced amount is too low, say an error has been made, a *debit note* will be sent by the supplier for the difference.

Some suppliers combine the invoice with the delivery note. In this case a credit note will be issued for any items returned or noted as missing at the time of the delivery.

Supplier's *statements* are similar to bank statements. They list as debits the various amounts invoiced in the last month (the typical period). Payments are shown as credits.

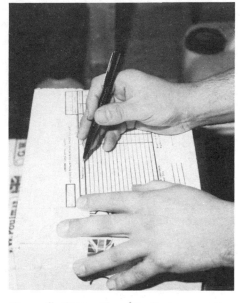

Generally three copies of the form are made, one is kept by the person making the order, one by the person issuing the items and the third is sent to the control office. If changes have to be made to the requisition, say some of the items are out of stock, the various copies should be amended. At least one copy should have the signature of the person receiving the goods

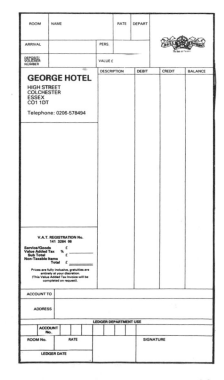

TO DO

One of the employees from the local printer arrives at a small hotel reception with 2000 guest bills and 3000 sheets of letterhead. The delivery also includes 500 plain envelopes but they are returned because they should have been overprinted with the hotel's logo and address. List, in the appropriate order, the documents which will have been completed from the time the stationery is ordered until the time it is paid for. (Assume the hotel has an account with the printers.)

The final impression customers form of an establishment will be influenced by the presentation of the various documents involved in obtaining and accepting payment.

Guest bills In a small hotel which uses manual accounting systems, the bill will be handwritten. Billing machines and computers have the advantage of speed but a printed bill tends to look impersonal and some guests find the symbols used to indicate the various categories of charge confusing. If the printer is one in which a continuous ribbon runs back and forth, the ribbon should be replaced regularly before the details on the bill become faint and difficult to read.

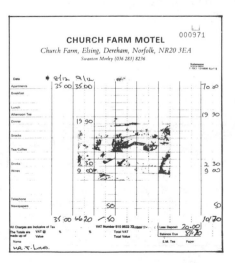

USEFUL TERMS

Debit Money paid out or an amount owed, always shown on the left-hand side of a set of accounts. For example a cheque drawn on a bank account, a charge made to a guest's bill for overnight accommodation.

Credit Money received or a positive balance in an account, always shown on the right-hand side of a set of accounts. For example payment into a bank account, payment by a guest of whole or part of the bill.

Details on the bill will include:

Pre-printed	Printed/handwritten
Name, address and telephone number of establishment	Date
	Customer's name
VAT registration number (unless the establishment is too small to pay VAT)	Room number if appropriate
	Description of charges
Serial number of bill	Amount of each charge
	Description and amount of any allowances or payments on account
	Amount of deposit paid
	Amount to be paid
	Amount paid
	VAT on amount paid
	Service charge on amount paid
	Method of payment

Calculators

Provided they are used correctly calculators will save much time when adding up figures, converting foreign currency, calculating percentages and so forth.

But it is best not to rely entirely on a calculator. If you use it incorrectly or press the wrong number by mistake, you get a completely wrong answer – and you won't even realise it if you have no idea of what the total should be. So, until you have got more experience of using calculators accurately and judging that the answer you have got is correct, it is best to do the calculation in your head (or on paper if it is complicated) and only use a calculator to confirm the answer.

 TO DO

Prepare your own example of a typical hotel bill to illustrate all the details it should include.

To make giving change easier and help avoid mistakes the cash drawer is divided into compartments for different notes and coins. At the beginning of the shift the drawer will contain a float made up of coins which are given to customers as change. At the end of the shift the total cash taken is balanced, minus the float of course. The amount of the float will vary according to what customers at that establishment are likely to need in change

Credit and direct debit card payments When a customer pays by credit card an imprint is taken of the card (see unit 46).

- This can be done on a small hand-operated machine when the card and a blank voucher are placed between guides and the roller pulled quickly back and forth, causing an impression of the card to form on the voucher. The date, a description of the charge and the amount is then handwritten on the voucher and the customer asked to sign it.

- A faster system works from the coded information printed in the black band on all credit cards. After the card has been fed through a slot on the top of the machine all the details including the amount are printed on a sales voucher (this looks like a cash till receipt) with a space for the customer's signature. Two copies are printed, one for the customer, one for the establishment. These machines are often linked to or are part of the point of sales equipment (or cash till to give it a more common name).

- The more sophisticated credit card imprinters are linked directly to the computers of the credit card companies. The customer is asked to sign the voucher while it is still on the machine. The payment is immediately processed (provided it is within the customer's credit limit) and a copy of the voucher torn off as the customer's receipt.

If a charge to a guest's bill is incorrect a correction, allowance or adjustment has to be made

Receipts In many cases a separate receipt is not necessary for hotel guests. When the bill is printed on a billing machine or computer a zero balance will indicate payment. Credit card vouchers also act as a receipt.

When the bill is handwritten the customer's copy can be rubber stamped 'Paid', or the person accepting payment writes 'Received with thanks' and signs or initials the bill. Alternatively a separate receipt can be written out. This should be from a numbered receipt book. (The numbering ensures every receipt is accounted for and prevents misuse of receipts and fraud.)

Cash received book

This book records all cash receipts and payments. It is mostly used when the front office deals with a wide range of cash transactions, not all of which are controlled by the tabular ledger or billing machine.

At any time (provided the entries are up to date) the balance shown in the cash book should agree with the actual money in the cash drawer (after the value of any float has been taken into account).

Many of the statistics used by management for forecasting, budgeting and planning are produced by the front office.

Occupancy   Occupancy levels are normally expressed in percentages of the full occupancy level. In a sports centre it would be the sessions during which the badminton court is used. In a hotel it would be the number, or rather proportion of rooms let on a certain day:

$$\frac{\text{Number of rooms let}}{\text{Number of rooms available}} \times 100 = \text{Room occupancy percentage}$$

For example

$$\frac{38}{65} \times 100 = 58.5\%$$

As most hotels have a variety of rooms – singles, twins, doubles and perhaps family rooms – occupancy is also measured in terms of the number of guests sleeping in the hotel on a particular night (compared in this case with the total number of beds available). Another way of measuring hotel occupancy is to compare the number of rooms occupied by two people with the total number available for two people. This gives useful background to the room occupancy figure when double or twin rooms are let for single occupancy.

Revenue   This is the total sales for a particular business day, week, month, four-week period or year. (Using a four-week period enables the year to be split up more evenly than a calendar month. There are 13 four-week periods in a year, 12 of 28 days and one of 29 days, making 365 days in all. In a leap year one period will have 30 days.)

Revenue details are kept for each of the main departments (see units 47 and 48). In this way more meaningful comparisons can be made with previous business periods and with forecasts, for example an increase in bar sales (which requires no action) will not obscure a decrease in restaurant sales (which should certainly be investigated and may require action).

Average spend   This is the total sales for a particular period divided by the number of customers. For hotel accommodation it will be the accommodation sales divided by the number of sleepers to get the average spend per guest, or when divided by the number of rooms occupied the average spend per room. In a restaurant it will be the food (and drink) sales divided by the number of customers or covers served.

Method of payment   Analysing what proportion (and/or value) of sales is cash, cheque, company account, Access, American Express, Barclaycard, Diners Club, company credit card (for example Trusthouse Forte's Goldcard) and so forth will help management plan cash flows (that is how much cash is actually available to spend at a particular time). It can also provide useful marketing information helping make decisions about advertising in credit card magazines, or even in persuading credit card companies to advertise in the establishment's own guest magazine.

The information in this unit will help you gain the Caterbase module *Producing Summary Statistics*.

How to calculate percentages, ratios, and averages and how to present statistical information is covered in greater depth in *Working in the Hotel and Catering Industry*.

USEFUL TERMS

Graph   A drawing indicating the relation between certain sets of data (typically two, for example the day of the month and the level of occupancy), usually by means of a series of dots, crosses or lines, plotted with reference to the horizontal axis (days of the month) and the vertical axis (different levels of occupancy). A scale (not necessarily the same) has to be chosen for each axis so all the data can be represented in an appropriate way.

Bar chart, bar graph or **bar diagram**   A graph consisting of vertical (or horizontal) bars whose lengths are proportional to amounts or quantities. (A density chart, see unit 11, is a form of bar chart. As bookings are taken the length of the bars increase.)

Pie chart   A circular graph divided into segments or sectors proportionate in size to the quantity represented.

Pictogram   A graph on which symbols are used to represent values such as the number of guests. One 'person' may be equivalent to ten guests, depending on the scale used.

Average length of stay This is another way of analysing trends and getting to know more about the customers. In a restaurant aiming at a high turnover of tables it is useful to know how long customers spend over their meal. If the average is 90 minutes and the restaurant is open from 6 p.m. to midnight, then it is theoretically possible for each table to be used four times. In resort hotels the average length of stay is significantly longer than it is in city centre hotels catering for business people, but not as long as it used to be when most families took one main annual holiday of two weeks and spent all the time in one place.

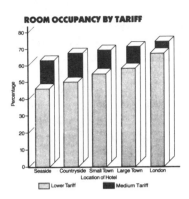

Rows of figures can be rather meaningless, even those which are considered very useful such as the occupancy levels of a hotel or the number of visitors to a tourist attraction. Converted to a bar chart the trends can be seen at a glance

Pie charts are an effective way of showing the relative importance of a number of elements. From this example it is quickly apparent where most of the attraction's visitors come from. A problem in that market – for example political uncertainty or an economic recession – would have a serious effect on the level of business, so a deliberate policy may be put in hand to develop other markets

Customer profile Information on the nationality of customers is available from the registration forms. Other information on customers can be built up by examining booking records, by asking specific questions when bookings are made, such as how did the person hear about the hotel, and by incorporating additional questions on registration forms such as reason for visit. The data can be used to market the establishment more effectively, for example by deciding to attract more visitors from France, then at a later stage measuring the results (in terms of increased numbers of French guests) of advertising, direct mail campaigns and other methods which might be used to reach the French market.

Forecasts These help management and heads of department plan staffing levels, decide on the timing of major redecoration programmes, control cash flows and stock purchases and generally ensure the organisation runs smoothly and meets its objectives. Forecasts can never be precise but they are a useful planning tool, drawing on past experience and established trends to predict future events, for example:

- wine sales over the next year
- the room occupancy next month
- laundry costs for the next six months.

 TO DO

Remember:

- statistics should be presented so that other people can understand them, not just the person who produced them
- the purpose of producing statistics is to focus attention where attention is required. (Some managements prefer to get 'exception reports' on a daily or weekly basis and only require full reports fortnightly or monthly.)

With these points in mind, choose two or three sets of statistics that are produced in the front office of your workplace, or an establishment of your choice. Display each set in two ways of your choice, say a bar chart and a pictogram. Show your work to some colleagues and ask them to tell you what they find the most effective method and why.

Carbon copying Inserted between two sheets of paper, carbon paper will copy the pressure of writing or of typewriter keys from the top sheet to the sheet below. The carbon paper is coated with a dark waxy substance which transfers to any suitable surface. A black impression is created, or dark purple depending on the type of carbon paper chosen. Although carbon paper is generally quite thin it can be used several times and still give a good reproduction of the original. A maximum of four or five copies can be made at the same time by inserting carbon paper between each sheet of paper, however the impression gets weaker and the bottom sheet can be difficult to read (see unit 17).

NCR paper This works in a similar way to carbon paper transferring an impression on to the next sheet of paper (or any surface immediately below). The copying substance is coated over the back of the paper which is written or typed on so it is not necessary to use carbon paper (hence the name No Carbon Required).

NCR paper is used for invoices, order forms, receipts and other documents which always require a certain number of copies. The copies (and sometimes the original) are on thin paper. Each copy may be pre-printed with specific information, for example 'Control office copy', and sometimes the copies are on different coloured paper. Documents printed on NCR paper are usually organised in sets with the top sheet and various copies collated in the appropriate order. Each set may be lightly glued together along one edge. When sets are supplied in pads a sheet of cardboard should be inserted before the next set otherwise writing will go through on to the wrong set of copies.

Photocopying Written, printed or graphic work is copied using a light-sensitive photographic process. Unlike carbon or NCR paper there is no limit on the number of copies that can be produced (most machines have a control panel for setting the number of copies required) and the quality of copies remains consistently high. Indeed the copies can be as good as the original and some copiers have a control for darkening or lightening, enlarging or reducing the original. Photographs generally do not photocopy well and if the original is printed on coloured paper the copy may be difficult to read.

Many different types of photocopier are available from small desktop models that produce acceptable copies of standard size documents, to large and sophisticated machines that operate at high speeds and produce excellent reproductions. The bigger models can handle different sizes of paper (typically A4 and A3 - see unit 17) as well as computer printouts. There is a second paper tray which the machine can be switched to for copies required on a different type of paper (letterhead, for example, or coloured paper). Copies can be made automatically from an original which is printed on both sides, to produce either single-sided copies or double-sided copies. The copied documents can be collated and even stapled.

Colour copiers are too expensive for most businesses to have their own but many photocopying shops now have the equipment and will make copies of coloured brochures, photographs, illustrations and so forth at a reasonable price.

The administrative aspects of reception work and the almost continuous process of sending and receiving information from other departments requires a large variety of documents to be copied, sometimes many times

 TO DO

Investigate the options available at your workplace or college for producing and copying a sales leaflet. Decide first what the purpose of the sales leaflet will be and how it will be distributed. If suitable facilities and equipment are not available in-house for the sort of project you have in mind suggest an external supplier and indicate the likely costs.

You now want to get the go ahead of your manager or tutor. Summarise your conclusions and recommendations in a brief report which you could show to the person concerned.

Faxing Facsimile machines work in a similar way to a photocopier except that the copy is produced in a different place or even a different country using the telephone network (see unit 14).

Some fax machines can be programmed to send copies of the same document to several different places at the same time. This can even be done out of hours when telephone charges are lower and the lines less likely to be engaged. The process is automatic, neither the sending nor the receiving machines need to be attended and if a receiving machine has run out of paper the document will be stored until the paper supply is replenished.

Spirit or ink duplicating This is now a rather old-fashioned method of making copies of documents. With some systems the original has to be prepared on a wax-coated master – using a stylus that cuts through the wax or typewriter keys (the ribbon is turned off). With other systems a master has to be made from the original using a special machine and materials. The master is then placed around a sort of drum on a small hand or electrically operated machine. As the drum rotates, it is coated with ink and brought into contact with the paper on to which the copies are made. The ink only transfers to the paper where there is a cut or indentation on the master.

The masters wear out after a time (a spirit duplicator can do up to 300 copies, an ink duplicator around 5000), but they can be used for a series of shorter runs. The masters must be stored away from dust and light, and hung up so they do not crease.

The quality of copies produced on duplicating machines is satisfactory for internal documents, minutes of meetings and so forth. In some establishments they are still used for printing menus.

Offset litho Some establishments have access to an in-house printing department, perhaps at company head-quarters or possibly their own if they are providing the catering service to a big organisation. Medium to large quantities of documents can then be printed economically and to high quality standards on an offset litho machine. The impression is made on to an intermediate surface such as a rubber blanket and then transferred to the paper. A coloured document is printed by making separate masters, one for each colour, and passing through the paper a number of times: twice for two colours, for example.

Controlling the issue of keys

To staff

A system of master keys avoids the need for certain people to carry keys for a large number of doors.

Grand master Opens every lock even if it has been double locked. The general manager, duty manager or other senior member of management will usually be the only person to be entrusted with a grand master.

Master Opens every lock but not one which has been double locked. The duty manager, executive housekeeper and chief security officer are the only people likely to be given a master key.

Sub-master and *floor* or *section master* will open locks on a particular floor or wing of the building unless they have been double locked. (These are also known as *section* or *pass keys*.)

A log book is kept with details of all key issues to management and staff. The date, time, name of person receiving the key and that person's signature are entered in the book. Similarly an entry is made on return of the key.

To guests

Hotel bedroom keys must never be given out without first checking the identity of the person requesting the key. In some hotels keys are only given out on production of a key card (see unit 13).

Computerised key systems are becoming commonplace in an effort to reduce theft and to minimise the expense and inconvenience caused when keys are lost or taken away by guests. The key either looks like a key (except that it is plastic) or a credit card punched with holes. The key and lock are programmed at the time the guest is first issued with the key. The program is unique to the guest and to the guest's room, so the key will not open any other door, nor will it work for the original room once the guest has checked out. If a guest loses the key the program is changed and a new key issued.

Security systems and equipment depend for their effectiveness on the people who use them. Take keys as an example. The best quality lock is no use if the key to it gets into the wrong hands, or is mislaid

Computer key systems are becoming increasingly sophisticated. Some will keep a record of what key has been used to open each door (for example the guest's key card or the card issued to the floor housekeeper) and when. Another system is designed to reduce energy costs. A certain time after the occupant has left the room the heating is automatically turned down and any lights left burning are switched off

1 Hold key with black magnetic strip on the left

2 Insert key in one smooth motion to activate green light on the lock

3 Wait for green light to go out

4 Turn key in the direction of arrow to open door

DO NOT leave your key in lock for any reason!! Keep this envelope with you as the key does not have your room number printed on it.

Protecting guest valuables

Many hotels have a number of safe deposit boxes where guests can leave their valuables. This gives the guest greater privacy and security than the alternative: to accept items for safe-keeping in the hotel safe.

- The deposit box can only be opened by using two keys at the same time: the key which has been issued to the guest and a master key held by the duty manager or head receptionist. A duplicate to the guest's key is kept in the bank in case the original is lost.
- Each time the guest uses the box a card is dated and signed and the guest's signature checked.
- The valuables are kept in a sealed envelope so that the contents remain unknown to the staff.

Luggage passes

When luggage is left for safe-keeping a pass or receipt should be issued to the owner. This will usually be numbered and a copy will be attached to each item of luggage. Alternatively the number can be written in chalk on the outside of suitcases.

The luggage should only be handed back when the receipt has been produced.

Security systems

Closed circuit television (often known as CCTV) to observe front and back public and staff entrances, delivery points, foyers and so forth. Cameras can be made to move, zoom in close on the subject, or carry out a continuous sweep of the area.
Invisible beams to span corridors, entrances, windows and so forth. When the beam is broken an alarm signal at the control panel shows the location of the problem.
Pressure pads fitted under carpets or floors at entrances, or in front of valuable objects, for example. An alarm signal is set off when someone stands on or walks over the pressure pad.
Sensors which can be set to pick up the vibrations caused by someone forcing a door or window, for example, but which ignore normal disturbances. Another type of sensor can pick up the heat radiated by a person.
Luggage scanners, firearm and *bomb detectors* are used extensively at hotels and conference centres which host occasions involving royalty, prominent politicians, diplomats, government ministers and so forth.

◆ ◆ ◆   **TO DO**

In a large hotel a person approaches the reception desk at a busy time. He asks for the key of 4215. The receptionist hands him the key then a few moments later asks in a rather surprised tone 'But that's the key to the President Suite?' The person immediately apologises and explains he meant to ask for the key of 4251.

A scene like this occurs in the film *Hotel* (based on Arthur Hailey's novel of the same title). The person is a professional hotel thief and the busy receptionist reacted exactly as the 'guest' planned. What do you think the thief was up to? If you were advising on a re-make of the film how would you bring this scene up-to-date? The original film shows the thief making off with a briefcase he finds in the President Suite. When he gets back to his own room he can hardly believe his luck – it's crammed full of money.

‼️   **REMEMBER**

You should never ignore a fire alarm just because you think it is false or a drill that you have not been told about. This time it may be a real fire. Prompt action saves lives. See unit 55.

The image the receptionist presents should conform to the image of the establishment itself. This may vary – from the formal, to the casual – but there are certain aspects of personal appearance and hygiene which should never be ignored whatever the circumstances.

Hair, face and hands Hair should be kept clean, neat and appropriately styled: preferably away from the face, with long hair tied back. Men should be clean shaven or keep beards and moustaches neatly trimmed.

If worn, make-up and jewellery should be used sparingly (the establishment's policy must be checked first). Special care should be taken to maintain a clear skin and complexion.

Hands and fingernails should be kept clean and well looked after. Hands must be washed regularly and thoroughly.

Personal freshness Any odour will be offensive to customers and work colleagues. Frequent bathing is important and strong scents, perfumes, after-shaves or colognes should be avoided.

Teeth should be regularly brushed and properly looked after. Bad breath should be counteracted with mouth fresheners.

Posture A tidy posture is controlled – not fidgeting and fussing. A smart posture is an upright one – not shuffling, with feet dragging. A good posture – when standing, walking or even sitting – has a good effect on customers and colleagues. It is also good for the figure and will help prevent corns, aches and pains.

Reception staff spend much of their time on their feet – good quality, strong shoes will prove far more comfortable (and safer!), especially at the end of a long day, than fashionable, lighter shoes. If possible, alternate pairs of shoes – some people find it helps to change shoes during the day.

!! REMEMBER

If you look good, you will have more self-confidence and are likely to feel good.

And if you feel more confident about the work you are doing so will your customers, your colleagues and your supervisors.

Your customers will be more satisfied with the services your establishment has provided.

Your colleagues will be able to do their jobs better because of the positive effect you have had.

Your supervisors will have more confidence in you and your chances of promotion within the company are increased.

On the other hand if you do your work in a sloppy way, dress in a sloppy way or wear your uniform in a sloppy way and don't keep it clean and well looked after, then you cannot blame your customers, colleagues and supervisors for believing that you are a discredit to the establishment. Always bear in mind that an untidy appearance instils uncertainty and anxiety, while a well-kept, smart appearance generates confidence.

The first people whom guests and other customers meet when they enter the premises are probably going to be the reception and front of house staff. What the staff look like – their clothes, hair, and general way of presenting themselves – is going to be crucial to the impression customers get of the entire establishment

Healthy living guide
Try and regulate the quantity and types of food and drink you consume, so that your body weight is in proportion to your height (your doctor will advise you).
- Eat less fat and avoid fats high in saturates, for example, butter and lard. Look for the label 'high in polyunsaturates' on fats and oils you eat and cook with.
- Eat less sugar and avoid drinks and foods which have a high sugar content.
- Eat more fibre. Choose whole grain cereals and bread in preference to highly refined white bread. Eat more pulses, fruit and vegetables.
- Eat less salt and avoid tinned and processed products that have a high salt content.
- Do not smoke and reduce alcohol consumption to moderation.
- Get sufficient sleep and take regular exercise.
- Try and include periods during the day when you can relax.
- Have regular medical and dental check-ups.

Care of your clothes Trousers, skirts, dresses, overalls and jackets should be hung up on clothes hangers to avoid unnecessary creasing which damages the fibres of the clothes and makes them look scruffy. Freshly laundered and ironed shirts may be hung up on hangers or carefully folded and placed in a drawer. Items such as cardigans, pullovers and scarves should be folded neatly to minimise creasing.

- Wash clothes frequently. Dirt builds up in the fibres, and may be hard to remove if left for a long time.
- Read the label giving washing instructions on the garment.
- Sort clothes according to the recommended wash.
- Soak if necessary to remove stains, but never soak wool or silk.
- Wash coloured clothes separately unless sure that the dye will not run.
- Check that the garment is colour-fast by placing a small section in water first.
- Use a soap which is suitable for the type of fabric being washed and enough to clean the item effectively. Some soaps are best for hand-washing, others for machine-washing.
- Rinse thoroughly.
- Fabric conditioner may be used to restore softness and to get rid of any remaining soap.
- Treat stains quickly.

Pockets

Pockets are for holding items essential to the job such as note pads and pens. They are not for holding any old item.

- Cramming tissues or other items into a pocket will cause a garment to lose its shape.
- Avoid placing pens in pockets unless the caps are firmly in place, or ink leaks may occur.
- Loose coins may cause a pocket to wear thin. Use a purse to carry change.

 TO DO

Under the heading *Presenting a clean and tidy appearance* make your own list of important points. Then take a good look at yourself – in a full length mirror if possible. Is there anything about your appearance – your hair, make-up, work clothes, hands – which you could improve upon? List these points, and during the following week make a special effort to make changes for the better. You will be surprised how good this makes you feel. You may wish to keep a count of the number of complimentary comments made by colleagues, friends and even customers!

Rules of stain removal

1. Try to identify the stain and the surface.
   - Note the appearance. Stains caused by pastes or thick liquids, such as paint, nail varnish and mud, are solid looking and caked on the surface of the fabric. Some stains caused by liquids, such as wine or tea, penetrate the material.
   - Feel the stain. Hardness may indicate lacquer or glue, while brittle stains could be sugar compounds (these often turn white when scratched). Some stains, such as new paint or toffee, are tacky.
   - Note the colour. Many stains have characteristic colours – blood is red but becomes brown with age, and may even look black.
   - Note the odour. Certain stains, such as amyl acetate perfume and salad dressing, have characteristic odours. All odours are more apparent when steam is applied.
2. Remove as much of the stain as possible before using any other treatment, but avoid rubbing it. If the stain is solid, gently scrape away the hardened build-up; if the excess is liquid, use an absorbent cloth to mop it up.
3. Always test the effect of any stain-removal agent first, by applying to a part of the surface which cannot be seen.
4. Always use the mildest treatment first. Start with cold water if you are not sure about the type of stain, because hot water or detergent may set the stain and make it impossible to remove.
5. Always treat the stain from the outer edges and work inwards, so as to avoid spreading it and making it larger.
6. If the stain is persistent, then try a harsher treatment, but avoid hard rubbing or using strong stain removal agents.
7. After cleaning, thoroughly rinse the stained area with cold water.
8. Leave the area as dry as possible.

GUESTCRAFT TIP

Deal with all stains as soon as possible. Once a stain has hardened or has seeped into a surface, it will be much more difficult to remove. Try the weak stain removers first (they are listed below in order of strength).
Ball point pen ink: 1. methylated spirits, 2. paint remover 3. hydrogen peroxide
Blood: 1. cold water, 2. ammonia, 3. hydrogen peroxide, 4. rust remover
Chewing gum: 1. trichloroethylene
Coffee or tea: 1. water, 2. acetic acid, 3. hydrogen peroxide
Egg: 1. soap, 2. digester ink (blue or black): 1. warm water with pads to absorb loosened colour, 2 ammonia, 3. hydrofluoric acid
Lipstick or nail varnish: amyl acetate
Perspiration: 1. warm water, 2. ammonia, 3. acetic acid, 4. hydrogen peroxide

The reception area, sometimes called the foyer or front of house, is the place most people pass through to get in and out of the building. It is the shop window of the establishment, so special efforts should be made not only to keep it clean and tidy but also to make it as attractive to customers as possible. Front office staff should keep any eye out for any mishaps such as a spilled drink. They may also be responsible for the minute by minute cleaning and clearing, and for informing the housekeeper whenever any cleaning outside the normal routine is required.

The reception counter

The reception counter should be kept clear of rubbish and arranged in a practical and attractive way:

- ashtrays emptied and cleaned regularly or when required
- ink blotters replaced as necessary
- pens always available for guests, with a good supply of stationery close at hand, for example registration and message pads
- documents relating to the day's activities ready to refer to: arrivals, departures, conferences, functions and other special events
- promotional material and information sources kept up-to-date and attractively displayed: brochures, tariff lists, leaflets on local activities and attractions
- internal telephone conveniently located in a place where people using it have some privacy and will not block other customers' access to the reception desk
- legally required notices properly displayed (see unit 49): limiting liability for guests' property and advertising minimum and maximum room tariffs
- promotional notices attractively displayed: menus, details of events in the establishment and the area
- magazines and other reading material regularly tidied and renewed so it is available for customers waiting in the foyer for some reason
- rubbish bins emptied regularly
- dirty cups, saucers and glasses removed swiftly after use (by the receptionist or by waiting or bar staff).

The reception area

Seats may be provided for guests in the reception area or at the counter itself. Some establishments prefer a more intimate reception area, with a desk or several desks where receptionists can sit with customers. Computer and other equipment generally on view at a reception counter are kept in an adjacent office.

- The reception furniture and seating should be kept tidy and in its proper position.
- Finger marks, stains and rubbish dropped by customers should be dealt with promptly.
- Public telephones should not be allowed to get untidy. A supply of notepaper will discourage callers from writing messages on the surrounding surfaces. Coin collecting boxes should be emptied regularly.

A good receptionist is able to tell guests about local amenities, beauty spots and tourist attractions, and will have information on transport, good restaurants (preferably the establishment's), and so on. He or she is always ready to attend to customers whatever other pressing problems there may be. Customers who get what they want are more likely to pay a return visit and tell their friends about the good service they received at the establishment. In this way opportunities to sell are increased

---

  TO DO

Choose a reception area you know and write a checklist of the tasks the reception staff have to perform to keep their workplace looking smart and attractive. Categorise the tasks according to how often each one has to be done, for instance:
- as required/after completing an operation or task
- daily/weekly/periodically, say every six months.

Alternatively

Buy or pick some flowers and attractive greenery and make your own arrangement. When planning the overall shape and appearance, bear in mind where you want to keep the arrangement, for instance on a table, in a corner or on the floor, and what sort of container you will be using.

Front of house is normally the area within an establishment used by more people than any other. With so many customers and staff moving to and fro every effort must made to prevent accidents from happening. And if an accident does occur the receptionist must know what to do – see unit 52

The good receptionist:
- is always well presented
- possesses a sense of humour
- has a warm and friendly personality
- works accurately and neatly
- is able to cope under pressure
- can sell the establishment's products and services
- shows tact and diplomacy in difficult situations
- apologises to a customer who complains
- never passes the buck
- remains calm even when customers are very angry
- does not interrupt the customer
- takes action promptly to put matters right
- ensures that what the customer has been told will happen does happen (or explains the reasons for any events which do not go to plan)
- checks regularly that customers are satisfied
- does everything possible to keep the customers satisfied.

 FOR INTEREST

In some establishments outside companies are contracted to supply and maintain indoor plant displays and provide all the floral arrangements. Alternatively a member of the house-keeping staff is responsible, or the reception staff will be in charge of the arrangements in their area.
- Choose flowers which are in season. Try simple, carefully proportioned arrangements and choose a container or vase which is easy to work with. Oasis, a substance available from florists, will help support your arrangement, and the oasis can be taped to the base of the vase to stop the whole thing toppling over. Elaborate arrangements are best left to the experts.
- Cut the flower stems diagonally at the required length. This enables the flower to absorb water more easily. Remove leaves and flowers from any part of the stem which will be covered with water. This helps prevent the water becoming stagnant.

- Check the water daily and top up as necessary. Water which is more than two or three days old, or which smells unpleasant, should be replaced with fresh water.
- Remove wilting or dead leaves and flowers regularly. Try to disturb the arrangement as little as possible.
- Keep flower arrangements out of direct sunlight and draughts, otherwise the flowers will die more quickly.
- Dried or silk flowers make an attractive alternative, particularly in winter when fresh flowers are more difficult and expensive to buy. They should be kept dust free. (Some local authorities insist that dried flowers are treated with a fire retardant.)
- Carefully chosen and well cared for potted plants provide a cool, fresh and natural look. Do not over water them and keep the leaves free from dust and insects.

Some people find communicating with others easy. Some find it more difficult. Whatever sort of personality you have, even if you think you are good at communicating with people, there is always room for improvement. And that takes practice and an understanding of what communication involves:

- speaking – verbal communication using the voice
- listening – aural communication using the ears
- body language – visual communication using the eyes.

Talking

Speech has certain characteristics which affect the message that is being spoken. For example 'Have a nice day' can seem insincere or even sarcastic, depending on how it is said, while it can and should be a friendly, sincere form of greeting that Americans in particular appreciate.

Volume Loud speech may sound bossy, very quiet speech cannot be heard.

Pitch An unnatural pitch usually sounds false so it is best for people with particularly high or deep voices not to try and disguise them. Some people's voices get higher in pitch if they become agitated or over-excited, this can turn into an irritating whining.

Tone Warm tones if overdone can sound grovelling, while cool tones are very unwelcoming.

Pace Fast speech is not easy to follow, but very slow speech makes the speaker sound stupid, or gives the impression that he or she thinks the listener is stupid.

Listening

People feel at ease and valued if they know they are being listened to. They will feel more confident and able to make their needs known. The listener gains too, learning more about the person talking – forming better relations with colleagues and providing a better quality service to customers. Considerable time and frustration is saved. Fewer mistakes are made.

Listening involves more than just what someone says. It is an active process:

- Full attention must be given to the speaker. It is no good letting the mind wander, or getting distracted by other goings-on.
- Interest must be shown in what the speaker is saying. Interruptions or attempts to upstage the speaker should be avoided.
- The important things the speaker is saying should be picked out and interesting but irrelevant detail ignored.
- Action must be taken on what has been said. If necessary notes can be made, or other staff fetched so they can take action.

It is a good idea to summarise information especially if it is communicated verbally. For instance, 'So that's a single room for two nights from April 19th, Miss Powers.' It could avoid confusion later

!! REMEMBER

It is better to know one or two words of a foreign language than none at all. Foreign customers appreciate the effort you are making to communicate with them in their own language.

The receptionist needs to communicate well with visitors and staff if the establishment is to run smoothly and customers are to be satisfied. Bad communication causes confusion, ill-feeling, time wasting, and in the extreme can cost the establishment dearly through loss of revenue and reputation

Body language

Three-quarters of all communications takes place without words through what is called body language. Becoming more aware of it and the way you and others use it will give you:

- more clues to your customers' needs
- more control over your own behaviour
- a better understanding of your work colleagues.

You can learn to read body language first by watching others and then trying to relate this to your own body language.

Facial expression The look on your face says a lot about your attitude and feelings. Most people will look at your face for a good deal of the time during a conversation, especially at your eyes. These, and your mouth, are the most expressive features of your face. So there is no point in saying:

'How lovely to see you again, Mrs Marley'

if you are trying to stifle a yawn, or the look in your eyes is dull and the corners of your mouth are turned down. This is why a smile can work wonders.

Gestures Everyone uses their hands to a greater or lesser extent to give emphasis to what they are saying. The way the head is held is also a great giver-away of true feelings and attitude. If a customer asks you where the lavatory is your guidance will be much clearer if you point and look in the appropriate direction. However using words in this situation is equally important, for instance, 'Yes, madam, it's down that corridor (pointing) on the right (pointing again) opposite the lift.' If you pointed and did not speak the customer would probably think you quite rude.

Gaze Look at the other person who is talking to you as well as when you are talking. It will make him or her feel you are really listening, and you will thereby also be able to read the person's expression and each of you will get your message across to each other more effectively.

Space Everyone needs their own personal space around them, and if this is invaded the person feels threatened. You will soon know whether you are standing too close to customers or staff because they will back off and look uncomfortable. Putting obstacles in the space between yourself and another person can say a lot about your own attitude, for instance a big desk, dark glasses, folded arms all indicate that you want to keep people at a distance.

 TO DO

Which of the following is the more effective communication?

I would like to book a room.	I would like to book a room.
Yes, madam, what type of room and when?	For tonight?
A single from April 19th for two nights.	No.
Certainly, madam. What name please?	When for?
	April 19th.
	It is for yourself?
	No.

In the example on the left the receptionist is asking what are called *open questions,* that is questions which encourage the customer to give more information about her needs. Open questions often start with *how, when, why, where or what?* Closed questions, such as those used by the receptionist in the example on the right, encourage yes and no answers. Notice how much more information is communicated within approximately the same amount of time in the first exchange. In addition the receptionist will have made the customer feel far more welcome through the manner of questioning.

Alternatively

List two or three expressions which a receptionist might use when dealing with customers, for instance, 'I feel sure the adult learners' swimming session at 10 a.m. is the one for you, Mr Moby' or 'You will find the massage room at the top of the stairs, through the fire door, and it's the second door on your right.' Then, if possible with a friend, practise saying each of these lines in various ways, for example: with a smile/grimace, without looking at the 'customer', while looking the 'customer' straight in the eyes, while looking at the 'customer's' midriff or left ear, while standing very close and also far away, while slouching/inclining the head, while busily doing something else, while sitting on your hands, in a loud voice/quiet voice. Discuss with your colleague what impression you made, according to the way in which you spoke.

Everyone needs their own personal space around them

Most businesses could not exist without the telephone. Initial enquiries and bookings are usually made through a phone call, and so the receptionist's voice is often the first contact a potential customer has with an establishment. So it is important to make the right impression.

Telephone techniques

1. Smile. The caller will not see you smile, but a smile will help you feel friendly, and in turn you will sound friendly.
2. Speak directly into the telephone mouthpiece, but don't shout. Don't eat, drink, or smoke while you are on the telephone.
3. Talk at a comfortable pace, using clear simple language. Avoid abbreviations and jargon unless you are certain that the caller will understand. For example, you might expect a member of staff to understand what a 'stayover' is, but an outsider won't know what you are talking about.
4. Use your normal accent – just be yourself.
5. Be patient – make allowances for people who have difficulty understanding you. You may have to repeat some things or say them in a different way.
6. Pay attention, concentrate and show that you care. Give all your attention to the conversation – do not be tempted to carry on two conversations at once.

Incoming calls
1. Always have a pencil and paper to hand, and a message pad.
2. Answer the call promptly. This creates a good impression. If you cannot, apologise for the delay when you speak to the caller.
3. Include in your opening remarks:
   Greeting 'Good afternoon'
   Identification 'This is Noshers Sandwich Bar'
   Offer to help 'May I help you?'
   Your company may have a standard form of greeting which you are expected to use.
4. Find out what the caller wants. Listen carefully, and don't interrupt. Ask questions to find out more. Find out the caller's name and company, and use it.
5. Make a note of important points such as the caller's name, and the main points of the conversation.
6. Give service: information, making an appointment or reservation, transferring a call, taking a message and checking the information with the caller.
7. Before you close the call, ask the caller whether there are any more questions or comments.
8. Thank the person for calling and say good-bye.
9. You may need to follow up the call. Do this promptly: carry out the necessary action, pass on a message, make a note in the reservations book, send a brochure, and so forth.

Outgoing calls
1. Prepare yourself. Know what you need to tell or ask the person you are phoning. Have all the information next to you, such as details of a booking, prices, dates, or special requests. It is irritating for the receiver if you have to

---

Misunderstandings are more easily made over the phone than face to face with the customer because:
- you cannot use body language, for instance gestures, to get across what you want to say
- you cannot read the other person's body language to help you understand what he or she means
- the telephone can distort the voice or you can get a bad line which makes it difficult to hear
- using the telephone costs money to the caller, yourself or the establishment.

 FOR INTEREST

If you are ringing a theatre booking office, airline or tourist office, the switchboard may be so busy it takes several minutes for the call to be answered. If there is an automatic queuing system for calls at least you will be dealt with in turn.

The information in this unit and unit 59 will help you gain the Caterbase module *Handling Telephone Calls.*

?? HOW TO

Leave a message on an answerphone
People still find themselves unprepared when an answerphone message explains there is no-one to take the call. But with a little thought and experience it is possible to leave a useful and informative message on the tape.

Remember there is no need to rush what you have to say, most answerphones give the caller plenty of time to leave all the relevant details. If you have prepared yourself for the call your message should be brief and to the point anyway.
1. Greet and identify yourself.
2. State the day and time of the call.
3. Outline the reason for the call.
4. Give any information, ask any questions you need to.
5. Give your number and the times you are available.
6. Repeat your number.
7. Thank the person.

break off in the middle of the call to find a document, for example.

2. Greet and identify. If appropriate, mention the company you represent.
3. Be clear and brief. Keep to the point.
4. Listen carefully to the reply.
5. Make notes of important information, particularly dates, times, names and prices.
6. Check. Repeat all information provided to make sure that it is correct.
7. Thank the caller for his or her help and follow up any necessary action.

Transferring calls
1. Make sure that you know who the call is for.
2. Let the number ring for a reasonable time. The person may be busy.
3. If there is no answer:
   • use the public address system (see unit 14)
   • bleep the person concerned (see unit 14)
   and if there is no reply to these, ask the caller if he or she would like to leave a message or speak to someone else (see unit 40).
4. If the line is engaged, ask the caller if he or she wants to leave a message or ring back later. Or you may take down the number and get the person to ring back as soon as possible. If a person is waiting to be connected to a busy line, every 30 seconds or so go back to the person and apologise for keeping him or her waiting. If the wait is becoming a long one renew the offer to take a message.

Some companies have a policy that staff should identify themselves by name when answering a phone call, for instance, 'Good morning. This is St Mary's Hotel. Janice Hopkins speaking.'

!! REMEMBER

• If the caller has a query you cannot answer yourself ask the person to hold while you find out the necessary information or inform them that they are being passed on to someone who can help. Never leave a caller waiting on the line without reassuring him or her that you are attending to the enquiry. If possible keep callers informed at all times of the steps you are taking to help them. Otherwise callers may think you have cut them off or forgotten about them which does not do the name of the establishment any good.

• Take care when giving out information, especially over the telephone when you have no way of checking the identity of the caller. Do not give any personal or private details about customers, staff or the establishment. This does not mean you have to be rude. 'I'm sorry that I can't help you but it is the policy of the establishment not to give out any information of a private or personal nature.'

• If you are dealing with an emergency call get the telephone number of the caller in case you are cut off (see units 52 to 55).

• Follow your establishment policy on transferring incoming calls to customers and staff. If the caller's name is established before the call is put through you can check whether the customer or staff member wishes to take the call. It also gives the person taking the call a few moments (often quite useful) to prepare for the conversation.

• Keep up-to-date with staff changes. A caller asking by name for the new sales manager will not be impressed if the reply is 'I'm very sorry but we do not have a guest by that name.' An internal telephone directory and perhaps an organisation chart will help place telephone calls with the right member of staff.

▶▶▶ TO DO

George Bailey has carefully prepared for his call to Nikki Papadopoulos. Identify in general terms what he is doing at each stage of the proceeds (for example greeting the person). Also note what follow-up action he might be taking.

Hullo, this is George Bailey from Mounds Leisure Centre ... Could I speak to Nikki Papadopoulos, please?

Hullo, is that Nikki Papadopoulos?

This is George Bailey from Mounds Leisure Centre. I'm returning your call about the county badminton competition next month.

Yes.... I see....What age groups will your students compete in?

Yes ... under 15s, under 18s, adults.

So that's three for the under 15s, five for the under 18s, and six for the adults? And the address? Lyle High School, Beech Lane?
Good. Thank you very much. Goodbye, Miss Papadopoulos.

Letters

Always deal with correspondence promptly. If you have to write a business letter, present the facts clearly so that your message is easy to understand. It is best to jot down a number of points, arranging them until you are satisfied with the presentation, and then draft an outline.

- Decide the purpose of your letter. Are you trying to give information, an explanation or instructions, or persuade someone to do something? Put yourself in the readers' position. Ask yourself what do they need to know?
- Plan the order of your letter. Decide what the reader needs to know first of all, then what next. Make each point separately in a new paragraph.
- Use the person's name in the greeting: 'Dear Mrs James' not 'Dear Madam' and close the letter 'Yours sincerely'. If you know the person you are writing to on first name terms, then the letter will begin 'Dear Mary' and close with 'Best wishes' on its own or in addition to 'Yours sincerely' or its options. If you do not know the name of the person, for example because you are writing to a new supplier to request information on equipment, the best solution is to use 'Dear Sir' or, preferably, 'Dear Sir or Madam' and end the letter 'Yours faithfully'. With sales letters a way of avoiding the rather cold and cumbersome 'Dear Sir/Madam' greeting is to use 'Dear Client' for example, or 'Dear holidaymaker'.
- Some people like to write in the greeting and closure by hand. If the letterhead is pre-printed with the name of the sender, for example 'Walter Thompson, Marketing Director' the typist will not need to put the name under the signature.
- Wherever possible the person who writes the letter and whose name is typed at the foot should sign the letter personally. If the letter has to be signed by someone else the letters p.p. are written in front by the signature – 'p.p.', which means per pro, indicates that the alternative signatory has been given the authority to sign in the letter –writer's absence.
- Lay out the letter clearly, neatly and symmetrically, with wide margins and equal spaces between the paragraphs. Choose a style and stick to it. If you like block paragraphs, leave a line space between each one. If you prefer to indent the first line of a new paragraph stick to the same indentation, five characters for instance.
- As each full-stop and comma represents a stroke on the typewriter keyboard, some people prefer to omit punctuation outside the main body of the letter. Whatever you decide to do be consistent. It looks untidy to have 'Ms. J. E. Francis' as part of the address, then a salutation 'Dear Ms Francis' and the writer's name as 'H O Read'.
- Dates can be written as 'April 1st, 1992', or '1st April, 1992' or 1 April 1992'. Use the same style for dates occurring in the body of the letter.
- If an enclosure is being sent with the letter, some indication should be typed at the foot of the letter, for example 'Enc', or else an asterisk in the margin opposite the text reference, or even a bright coloured sticker. The purpose is to make sure that the enclosure is indeed enclosed. It also alerts the person receiving the letter (who may not have opened the envelope) that there should be an enclosure.
- Do check that the letter is free of errors before signing and posting it. Some people find it quite difficult to spot errors in typed material but this is no consolation to the customer addressed as 'Ms Frances' in one place and 'Miss Francis' in another. It is a common mistake to concentrate on checking the body of the letter only casting a quick eye over the address and so forth. If anything errors are more likely to occur in the address. A mis-spelled name is irritating to the recipient, an error in the address is likely to be copied on to the envelope and could mean the letter never gets to the intended person.
- If you are replying to a letter with an important reference, quote the reference in your reply. The reference on Ms Francis' letter is a common one, but not particularly useful for filing or any purpose other than to indicate who typed it (a person with the initials RAH).
- Whatever you say or write, choose words that are easy to understand. Why say 'I am of the opinion' when you can say 'I think', or 'commence' when you can say 'begin'? Expressions like '7th instant' are old fashioned and unnecessary as it is just as easy to say '7th March'. Many people don't believe the rather formal 'Assuring you of our best attention at all times'. You want your communication to be uncomplicated and easy to understand. Some people think that 'big' language impresses. It doesn't, and in many situations it may actually confuse.

Communicating effectively in writing is an important aspect of the receptionist's job, whether it be:

- letters or messages to customers
- messages, memos or reports to management and other staff

MEMORANDUM

DATE <u>4 March</u>
TO <u>Executive Housekeeper</u>

FROM <u>Head Recep</u>

SUBJECT: STAFF TRAINING

As agreed at the heads of department meeting on March I have arranged for the two new members to spend a day working in the housekeeping de

Miss Janet Adams — Tuesday, 20 March
Mr Frances Meganathan — Thursday, 22 March

I have explained that the aim is for them to get an insight into the procedures and method of working of all your staff, and that they will be expected to help with various tasks from cleaning bathrooms to inspecting rooms. As agreed they will report for duty at 7.30 a.m.

Sunny Cliff Tops
CARAVAN AND CHALET PARK

April 1st 19
Ref: HOR/RAH

Ms. J. K. Francis
245 London Road
Sudbury
Middlesex
2RY RHF

Dear Ms. Francis,
Thank you for your recent letter enquiring about booking a caravan holiday next summer. I am pleased to inform you that the third week in July and the second and fourth week in August are available. I am enclosing a brochure about the site and its facilities, and also our rates for next year. If you decide to book before the end of April I can offer you a 5% discount.
If you have any further questions, please do not hesitate to contact me.

Yours sincerely,

Harry Read

H. O. Read
Reservations Manager

DATE: July 8th...... **REQUISITION**
DESCRIPTION DEPARTMENT
09321

ACCIDENT REPORT FORM

Name of injured person *John Lewis*
Section/Department *Housekeeping* Occupation *House porter*
Supervisor/Manager *Jennifer Jenkins*
Time of report *9.30 am*
Time of accident *8.50 am* Date of report *April 19th*
Nature of injury *Twisted right ankle* Date of accident *April 19th*

Was hospitalisation required? *Yes - for X Ray*
Place of accident *Corridor - 4th floor*
WHAT HAPPENED (include equipments/items etc., and other persons)
J. Lewis tripped over the trailing flex to a vacuum cleaner which was left plugged in.

Witness evidence 1
Witness evidence 2
Supervisor's recommendations *Implement a training course for housekeeping staff on 'safe working practices'.*

Signature *N. Lewis*

be sent to the company health and safety officer

Messages should always be written down. It can be too easy to convince yourself that you will remember all the details, and then when the time comes you leave out a vital fact. Or worse still, you forget to deliver the message until much later, when it is too late. On the other hand, written messages will make sure you don't forget the details. Written messages are also permanent, so they can be referred back to – see unit 40

For: *Charlotte Banning* From: *Jennifer Hocking*
Date: *Tuesday January 12th* Time: *3.10pm*

Please can you meet me at Holly Tea House tomorrow at 3.30pm. If you can't ring me on 921-4440, otherwise see you there.

Message Taken By: *Dan (Telephonist)*

---

9 The Lane
London W5 5TB

15th June

Dear Sir,
I would like to make a reservation for my family and our dog. The dates I have in mind are August 1st to August 15th. Could you please let me know whether you have two rooms available for these dates? We would like one room for me and my husband, and another for my two children, aged 14 and 11. Also, can you let me know what arrangements you have for dogs?

Yours faithfully,

A.B. Jenkins

(Mrs) A.B. Jenkins

To/ Next Shift Date - March 9th 19...
Time - 3pm

1) *Mr and Mrs Pickering telephoned to say their train has been delayed – they will be arriving approx 8pm – so save their room.*

2) *The group from Japan will be leaving at 10pm instead of the next morning.*

3) *Make sure Room 212 gets the VIP flowers and fruit before 6pm when Ms. Costello arrives*

Head Receptionist

TO DO

Draft and then type (or if this is not possible carefully handwrite) a reply to the letter from Mrs Jenkins opposite. Before you start decide what are the main points requiring an answer, and what additional information you need to obtain from Mrs Jenkins, for example:

- Do Mr and Mrs Jenkins require a double or twin-bedded room?
- Does the family require accommodation for the night of August 15th (it is not entirely clear from her letter)?

In order to receive a telex or fax both parties have to possess similar equipment (see unit 22), and so it is usually with businesses rather than individuals that faxing and telexing will be done.

Telex and fax machines overlap in their uses, but there are occasions when one should be used rather than the other, for instance when:

- you want to send illustrations – use the fax
- you want to have a simultaneous conversation (message, answer, follow-up response) – use the telex
- the company you want to send to possesses only a fax or only a telex
- the document is already prepared for you – use the fax
- the information needs to be typed – use the telex or type the message on an ordinary typewriter or word processor and then fax it.

With telex machines you can hold a simultaneous 'written' conversation with the person at the other end. You type out and send your message and you can receive an answer in written form in the time it takes the other person to type out the words.

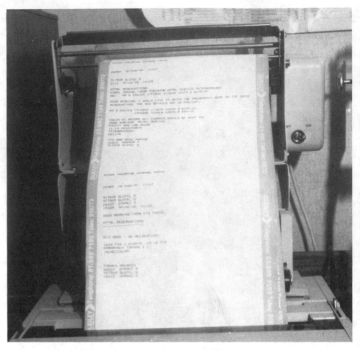

When sending a telex you type it out on the teleprinter itself. When sending a fax you need to have the document ready beforehand

The telex and fax are as quick as an ordinary telephone conversation, but they have the advantage of providing the sender and the receiver with a written (and illustrated in the case of a fax) record. This makes it less likely that the information will be misunderstood

?? HOW TO

Send a telex

1. Find the number you require – from the company's letterhead, business card or from the telex directory.
2. Tell the machine you wish to send a message – this may involve turning it on, or pushing a particular button.
3. Dial the number – if the connection is successful the answerback code will be printed out in front of you.
4. Send your answerback code – this will print out at the receiving end. (Answerback codes are the telex method of identifying the sender and receiver, usually a combination of a word and figures.)
5. Send your message. If it is a short message or you are having the equivalent of a conversation by telex, your printer and the receiver's printer will print the message at the speed you type it. For most messages it saves time to prepare the message before making the connection. The machine will store it until required, and once started transmission is very fast.
6. If you require an answer immediately, press the bell key and this will alert the operator at the other end. (Telexes do not need to be attended when receiving a message.)
7. At the end of the transmission give your answerback code then press the 'Who are you' key to get the answerback code of the receiving machine. This exchange is a useful check that the connection has not been cut during the call.
8. Where possible use the standard abbreviations (understood throughout the world) to cut the length, and therefore the cost, of telex calls:

ABS	office closed	CRV	is the message being received clearly?
DER	out of order	EEE	error
NOM	waiting	OCC	engaged
RPT	repeat	SVP	please
WRU	who is calling?	+	end of message

▶ ▶ ▶ TO DO

Write out a telex from a real life company whose number you find in the UK or International telex directory making an overnight reservation at a hotel. Then write a telex in reply as though you were the hotel receptionist dealing with the booking.

Telex and fax make it quite easy to organise travel and accommodation arrangements for visitors to the country

?? HOW TO

Send a fax

1. Find the fax number you require – from the company letterhead, business card or from the fax directory.
2. Place the document to be sent face down in the machine or have the document close to hand (depending on the type of machine).
3. Dial the number.
4. Adjust the controls (if available) for light or dark originals.
5. When the machine indicates the connection has been established, press the transmit button. Each page of the document will automatically feed through the machine.
6. Once the transmission has been completed the call will terminate (usually automatically). Some machines produce a printout giving the time and duration of the call, the number of pages sent and the fax number which was called.

Everyone working in hotels, catering, tourism and leisure needs to be able to work with other people, the receptionist perhaps more than anyone else. Front of house is the centre of communications for the entire establishment, and good working relations with colleagues, other departments, management and contractors (for instance builders, decorators, electricians) are essential if high standards of customer care are to be maintained.

Avoid being late for work because the previous shift cannot go home until the next shift arrives and the handover has been completed. It will cause friction among colleagues and ultimately show in the service provided for the customer. If you are unavoidably delayed or ill get a message to your workplace as soon as possible so that the necessary arrangements can be made to cover for you.

Housekeeping Guests who are departing and arriving, whether rooms are to be taken out for periodic cleaning, what special requirements guests have.

Restaurant Customers who have booked tables, any large parties arriving, cancellations of bookings.

Kitchen Any large parties arriving, special food requirements for guests, patients and customers, compliments from customers to the chef.

Maintenance Best times to decorate the swimming pool area, renew the reception carpet.

Working with colleagues

Colleagues should support each other. If one of you is under pressure, for instance a queue of guests has formed all wanting to check out, it may be possible for someone else in reception to lend a hand. This help, if freely and cheerfully given, will no doubt be reciprocated at a later date. The guests too will have received faster and more relaxed service because the person responsible for checking them out will have had some of the workload lifted.

Working with supervisory and management staff

Your immediate boss and those above need to know that they can rely on you. Part of their job is to delegate jobs to you, and they need to know that you can follow instructions as well as complete your normal tasks satisfactorily. No one does a job perfectly every time, and it is important to be able to accept criticism when due from the person in charge. Positive criticism is not meant personally but to improve working standards and customer care.

 TO DO

Each member of staff is dependent on others for the successful completion of his or her job. Here are two general activities in which teamwork is important. Discuss them and any other examples you can think of, with colleagues.

- Equipment will be used by a number of different people and it is important that each person keeps it in the appropriate condition for the next user.
- People who do their job badly make extra work for others. This is especially true when the responsibility for doing any one particular task varies from day to day, shift to shift.

Positive versus negative thinking

Being positive is really an attitude of mind. Positive thinkers make a habit of looking on the bright side no matter how difficult the situation. They choose to do so – it is a quite deliberate, conscious process. For a negative thinker to become a positive thinker means changing from what is really an easier route to follow – it take so little effort to slip into moodiness, to let minor irritations grow into major problems.

You have it in your power to influence the way people respond to you. If you have a positive attitude towards your work, friends and family they are more likely to have a positive attitude towards you. Next time a colleague, friend or member of your family is very busy and you have time to spare, offer to help them. See what reaction you get

> Say the housekeeper tells the receptionist that a mistake has been made and the flowers for a VIP arrival have been delivered to the wrong guest, room 332 not 323.
>
> The positive way out of this problem is to immediately arrange for the VIP to have something better. Get a bottle of champagne and a box of handmade chocolates delivered with a personal note from the general manager, for example (the cost will not be much more).
>
> The negative solution is to blame the housekeeper, complaining that the same mistake seems to keep happening. In turn the housekeeper blames reception, and is able to point out that the error came from the arrivals list. Someone is sent to remove the flowers from 332, offering as the only explanation to the guest 'They made a foul up!' By the time the VIP gets the arrangement one of the central roses has been broken at the stem.

Negative statements can be turned into positive statements with a little thought and effort.

Negative	Positive
Sorry sir, but the car park is full, and there is nothing we can do	Oh, I am sorry, Mr West. I know it is most inconvenient. Here is a complimentary ticket for the Grand Hotel car park one street north of here. If you would rather, I can ask the porter to park your car
Beaujolais Nouveau is off	May I suggest the excellent new wine from Australia as an alternative? It is made in a similar style and costs the same price. We had an unexpected party in last night and they got through our last stock of Nouveau until Monday's delivery

Being assertive

Even for a normally positive thinker, it is quite hard to deal with people who are rude, shout, get angry, interrupt you, blame you or keep you waiting. Faced with this sort of problem, some people give way submissively, others act aggressively.

The middle course is to openly, directly and honestly express your point of view, and show that you understand the other's point of view.

Submissive	Aggressive	Assertive
It's only my opinion but	That's absolute rubbish	I think
Oh dear, well it doesn't really matter	You must pay for the damage	We could get our respective insurance companies to inspect the damage, and then . . .

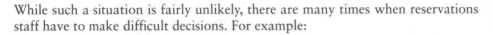

31 DEALING WITH

Every establishment has its own particular reservation procedures to make sure that important details are not overlooked or errors made. And each establishment has a certain amount of services and facilities available, and hopefully, a certain number of customers who wish to use them.

The aim is to match services and facilities available with the needs of the customers and the aims of the establishment

> Say a hotel's accommodation consists of 30 twin-bedded rooms. If a tour operator books all the rooms for a particular night for a group of 60 people the tour operator is well satisfied, but the hotel owner may not be.
>
> • The tour operator is likely to be paying a lower price per person than the hotel's normal tariff. The hotel would make a bigger profit if every room was sold at the normal rate for a twin-bedded room.
> • The hotelier might have to turn away regular customers, and if these customers decide to try a competing hotel, it is possible they will never return.

While such a situation is fairly unlikely, there are many times when reservations staff have to make difficult decisions. For example:

> • There are no single rooms left and a regular customer books accommodation for herself for two nights. If the hotel's policy is applied of charging the full rate for a double room when it is let for single occupancy, the price may be over what the customer's company allows its staff. If the customer has to pay the excess herself she is not likely to want to use the hotel again.
> • The hotel is fully booked and a businessman arrives at reception and asks for a room for three nights (he has no reservation). In fact one customer with a confirmed reservation has not yet arrived. It is just after the official release time but severe traffic delays in the area may be the reason.

General procedure

Certain information must be exchanged at the time a reservation is made to ensure the customer receives prompt and efficient service at every subsequent stage, not only on the particular visit but on future visits.

 ▶ ▶ ▶ TO DO

Study the list of information required at the time a reservation is made. Not every establishment will want the same details so make your own checklist of information that should be obtained from the customer and from the establishment. Base it on a situation of your choice, say a small guesthouse in a tourist town, or a large hotel at a popular seaside resort. Then describe two examples of how something could go wrong if certain information was not obtained, or the details were taken down incorrectly.

From the customer		*From the establishment*
full name	estimated time of arrival	type of rooms available
home address and/or business address	any special requirements	type of accommodation reserved, the price and what the price includes
telephone number (home and/or business)	how payment will be made	name of person taking booking
name and contact details of person making booking (if different)		reservation number
company or travel agent details		date booking was taken
source of booking		what the customer has to do to confirm the booking
date of arrival		release time/guarantee or reservation
date of departure		advice on any facilities the customer should book in advance
type of room required		any special help which is required, such as a map showing how to get to the establishment
number of persons in party		alternative suggestions if the establishment is full/offer to waitlist
number of rooms required		
names of other members of party		
ages of children		

Filing correspondence

For every reservation a considerable amount of paperwork will be generated: letter of enquiry, reservation form, deposit required, amendment slip if booking changed, registration form and so forth. This needs to be filed in case there is a query at any stage and certain documents such as the registration form are kept for 12 months or longer after the time of the stay. Various filing systems are used (see unit 57), but a typical procedure is to:

1. File under the date of arrival
2. Keep the correspondence for each day's bookings in alphabetical order by name of customer
3. Place the most recent correspondence on top
4. Staple all the correspondence from one customer together
5. Place cancellations at the back of the file.

So paperwork relating to a booking from Mr and Mrs Carson arriving on March 4th is filed under that date.

> In some establishments unconfirmed bookings are filed separately. Another variation is to file one copy of the reservation records in a master file in alphabetical order by customer name and a second copy under the date of arrival.

So the Carson correspondence is placed after details of the Bovis Group booking.

So the Bovis confirmation letter is placed in front of the telephone record of the reservation.

This makes it easier to find details relating to a particular reservation and reduces the risk of important pieces of paper getting misfiled.

The information is then available if further action has to be taken, but without confusing the more important part of the file.

Amending bookings

- Find the records of the original booking.
- Take details of the change.
- Check availability if extra or different accommodation is required, or the dates of the booking have changed.
- Ask the customer to reconfirm the booking (if the change is made by telephone).
- Change the booking records on the chart, diary or computer. Complete an amended booking slip if appropriate.
- File details of the change. If the date of arrival has changed this will mean moving the file to the new date.
- Confirm the changes to the customer.
- Notify other departments as necessary.

The information in units 31 and 32 will help you gain the Caterbase module *Taking Reservations*.

> Many hotels do not charge when a booking is cancelled by the customer unless the notice given is so short that it is impossible to relet the room. Some holiday hotels operate cancellations policies similar to those enforced by airlines and tour operators, a percentage of the total price is charged, increasing to 100% if the cancellation is made at the last moment.

Cancelling bookings

- Find out when the booking was made for and in what name.
- Check the reservation record to confirm the details (so there is no risk of cancelling the wrong booking).
- Note the name of the person cancelling the booking and if it is different from the person who made the booking get contact details in case there is a query later.
- Give the person a cancellation reference number (if this is establishment policy). This will help distinguish genuine cancellations from those customers who are trying to avoid paying the bill for accommodation they booked but did not use.
- Note this reference number, the date the cancellation was made and the name of the member of staff who took the cancellation.
- If a deposit has been paid some or all of it may have to be refunded.
- Ask the person cancelling if an alternative reservation is required. If not say you are sorry that the person will not be able to stay at the establishment on this occasion, but you hope to have an opportunity of welcoming her or him in the future.
- Remove the booking from the diary, chart or computer reservation records.
- Mark the correspondence relating to the booking 'cancelled' and file.

When a reservation is made by telephone or in person it is much easier to make suggestions which will be helpful to the customer, and to clarify exactly what the customer requires. It may also be possible to persuade the customer to book a higher standard room or additional facilities (see units 9 and 10). Written requests for a reservation can lead to a lengthy exchange of correspondence if, for example, the customer has not been clear about the length of stay, or if the hotel does not have exactly what the customer has asked for. In all types of reservation, written confirmation is important to establish that a contract has been made (see unit 50).

Telephone bookings

- Work carefully through the list of details required from the customer (see unit 31) or make sure the standard reservation form is fully completed (see unit 12).
- Be very clear on what is being requested. Repeat the details if you are unsure on any point.
- If what the customer asks for is not available, offer the nearest alternative.
- If no acceptable alternatives can be offered, offer to waitlist the customer or suggest a nearby hotel in the same company or consortium (or with whom there is a good working relationship). With some computer reservation systems it is possible to make a booking in another hotel.
- If payment is by credit card or company account or a deposit is being paid, offer a guaranteed booking and take details over the phone. Explain the booking will then be automatically held until check-out time the next day, and the customer will be charged if he or she does not take up the booking.
- Ask for confirmation by letter, fax or telex as appropriate, and if necessary give a date by which the booking must be confirmed or the accommodation will be released for re-sale.
- Explain that a confirmed booking will be held until 6 p.m. or whatever the release time is. (For later arrivals, some establishments will insist that the booking is guaranteed.)
- Explain the procedure for cancelling a guaranteed or confirmed reservation.
- Offer to book other hotel facilities such as a table in the restaurant for dinner.
- Repeat the details of the reservation to the customer: name, address, date of arrival and date of departure (this is less confusing than stating the booking is from August 11th to 13th inclusive – some customers may think this means accommodation is booked for three nights, the 11th, 12th and 13th, not two nights, the general understanding), type of room booked, method of payment, special requests, estimated time of arrival, and need for confirmation or deposit.
- When entering the reservation details on the chart, in the diary or computer add a note on whether it is to be confirmed or is a guaranteed booking.
- File the booking form with the correspondence for the day of arrival.
- When the confirmation letter arrives note on the letter that it has been confirmed, attach the letter to the top of the reservation form and refile.

Personal bookings

The procedure is similar to that used for telephone bookings, but being face-to-face with the customer the receptionist has the chance to observe the customer's reactions and respond more sensitively.

- The reservations confirmation slip can be given to the customer directly.

A telex or fax greatly speeds up the process of dealing with written bookings requests. Telex offers the opportunity to ask and reply to questions immediately

‼ REMEMBER

- Some customers who telephone or come in person to make a booking know exactly what they want and also exactly what information the establishment needs to have. They do not want to take any longer than necessary over the call.
- Other customers need much more help especially if they do not speak English well, and are not sure what the hotel can offer, or are unfamiliar with some of the reservation terms and industry jargon.

- If payment is to be made by credit card, an imprint can be taken of the card and the guest asked to sign the voucher (for a guaranteed reservation).
- If a deposit is required a receipt can be given to the customer directly.
- The customer can be shown a room of the type booked, the restaurant menu and other hotel facilities.

Written booking requests

- If the type of accommodation or the dates requested are not available, offer alternatives which seem most closely to suit the customer's requirements.
- If the letter is merely an enquiry or the required accommodation is not available and an alternative is being offered, explain that a provisional reservation has been made which must be confirmed by a certain date or the accommodation will be released. A legal contract exists once an offer is accepted, so an additional qualification may be useful such as 'and provided the accommodation is still available at the time of receipt of your reply' (see unit 50). Ask for any additional information at the same time, such as time of arrival and method of payment.
- If the reservation is from a private individual or a company which the establishment knows nothing of, it may be the policy to ask for a deposit.
- When the letter of confirmation arrives note the fact in the reservation record.
- Confirm the definite details back to the customer.
- Letters to companies should make clear the arrangements for paying if the company does not have an account.

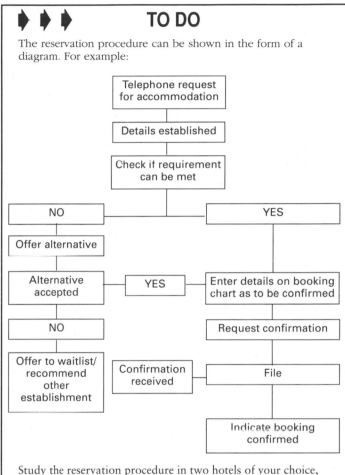

▶ ▶ ▶ TO DO

The reservation procedure can be shown in the form of a diagram. For example:

Study the reservation procedure in two hotels of your choice, one that uses a manual system and one that is largely or entirely computerised. Draw a diagram for each to show how a typical written reservation is dealt with.

USEFUL TERMS

Confirmed reservation Booking confirmed by letter, telex, fax, telegram or telemessage. If the customer does not take up the booking the establishment has written proof of the contract should it wish to pursue a claim for compensation from the customer.

Guaranteed reservation The customer guarantees the reservation, agreeing to pay whether the facilities booked are used or not. This makes it easier for the establishment to claim compensation if the customer fails to arrive.

No show A customer with a reservation who fails to take up the reservation or to cancel it.

Overbooking The practice of accepting more reservations than the establishment can actually accommodate. A careful calculation is made of the proportion of customers who book but do not arrive or cancel their reservation. This will indicate the 'safe' level of overbooking.

Overstays Customers who continue their stay beyond their original departure date.

Understays Customers who leave before their original departure date.

Chance arrivals or **walk-ins** Customers who arrive at the establishment without a reservation on the chance that suitable accommodation will be available.

Bookings made on behalf of customers

When reservations are made by a third party acting on behalf of the customer the process is generally easier and faster. Travel agents, hotel booking agents, other hotels in the company or consortium and so forth are all experienced at dealing with reservations. They will have all the necessary information to hand and be able to provide most of it unprompted. Confirmation will follow quickly by telex or fax. Or the whole process may be handled by computer, for example from a central booking office. What varies is the commission arrangement and the payment instructions.

Commission Travel agents and hotel booking agents are running a business and their reward for putting customers in touch with the providers of accommodation, transport and so forth is a commission, for instance 10% on the basic value of the booking. This might be for accommodation only or for dinner, bed and breakfast. Commission is not usually paid on extras the customers order once they arrive, such as drinks. The commission rate is negotiated in advance with the provider of the service.

Payment procedure Some agents only provide a booking service. The customers are responsible for paying their own account at the time of their stay. The commission will be calculated at this stage and forwarded to the agent shortly afterwards, or on a monthly basis, for example, if the agent regularly deals with the establishment. Other customers pay the basic accommodation charge in advance to the agent. In due course this is paid to the hotel, less commission. Any extras are paid direct to the hotel by the customer. The third option is for all the whole bill to be sent to the travel agent for payment, less commission.

There will not usually be a commission on bookings made by other establishments in the company, by the company's central booking office, if there is one, or by fellow members of a marketing consortium. There may be a direct computer link for inter-company bookings, so that a receptionist in one hotel can book accommodation for a guest in another hotel by accessing that hotel's computer reservation system. However if the reservation is for the same day, or the guest requires a special rate for example, it is best to phone the hotel concerned and explain these circumstances.

Reservations for groups

Group bookings are likely to be made by tour operators. They are often made a considerable time in advance, when the tour operator plans the year or season's itineraries. Sometimes they may include periods where a new group arrives each time a group departs (known as back-to-back reservations). If these plans are over-ambitious the tour operator may combine two groups into one, for example, and make cancellations of whole bookings. These can leave the hotel in some difficulty so an agreement should be made when the original booking is taken on when a tour can be released if not confirmed. For a reliable tour operator who has demanded a modest discount the booking may not be released until a week or so before the date. In other cases it could be up to 21 days in advance. The contract with the tour operator might also give the establishment some or all of the following rights:

‼ REMEMBER

When accepting a reservation from an agent check the payment instructions carefully. The agent will not accept responsibility for any payment not mentioned on the claims voucher (or whatever system is used for claiming payment from the agent).

Check commission claims carefully to avoid losing revenue to the establishment and damaging relations with the agent.

- Did the guest arrive and stay the number of nights claimed?
- Does the room rate on the claim agree with what the guest was charged?
- Has the commission already been paid/claimed?

◆ ◆ ◆ TO DO

You are asked to explain the different telephone tones to a member of staff who has just arrived in the country for the first time – a lot of telephoning is done in your establishment and many calls are to travel agents and tour operators whose numbers are quite often busy. Write a brief description of each tone which will act as a reminder to your colleague:

Dialling tone   Ringing tone
Engaged tone   Number unobtainable
(number called is busy)
Equipment engaged
(lines or exchange equipment busy)

- to amend prices in the event of a change of VAT rate or unforeseen changes in the cost of labour, for example
- to charge a supplement if over a certain percentage of the original number of bookings are cancelled
- to make a cancellation charge if a particular tour is cancelled within so many days before arrival
- to receive confirmation of the number of persons on a tour within 14 days of arrival, for example
- to receive a deposit at the time the booking is confirmed and payment of the balance within 30 days of the invoice date.

Some group bookings are made by one person acting on behalf of the group. For example the secretary of a company booking accommodation for the senior management's annual strategy meeting, or the chairman of a branch of the British Association of Barbershop Singers booking accommodation for the branch's representatives at the next annual convention. The names of individual guests may not be available until a few days before they are due to arrive and in this case the rooming list will be left to the last minute.

Another type of group booking is that made by airlines for their crew (and sometimes travel agents for their couriers). Rooms are reserved for the crew, say every Tuesday and Thursday for the next 12 months. If for some reason the crew do not take up the accommodation the airline will still be liable to pay (depending on the details agreed in the contract). So at very busy times, if the hotel discovers that the flight has been delayed and re-lets the rooms its occupancy percentage will be over 100%.

The information in units 31 to 34 and 21 will help you gain the Caterbase module *Consolidating Reservations*.

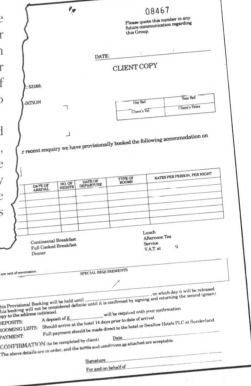

Reservations for conference/ meeting rooms

Front office staff may be required to handle reservations for conferences, meetings and interview rooms. If there is a requirement for special catering services, as would be the case for a wedding, for example, the person in charge of banquets, functions or food and beverages will be involved in the detailed discussions that are necessary. Establish:

- what time the room(s) will be required
- how many people will be attending
- what furniture layout is required
- when coffee and tea should be served
- if a table reservation is required for the restaurant
- what equipment is required, for example flip charts, video recorder and monitor
- who will be responsible for paying the bill.

Overbooking

Some hotels deliberately overbook in periods of peak demand. Their managers and staff are under pressure to meet room revenue targets and the hotel only has a certain number of rooms. Unfortunately an extra room cannot be sold the next night to make up for an empty room caused by a late cancellation or no show so a calculated risk will be taken at busy times and if the hotel has 100 rooms, for example, reservations will be accepted for 105 rooms. Past experience will show that a certain proportion of potential guests cancel at the last minute or simply fail to turn up (5% in this example). But if a poor judgement has been made and the hotel does not have a room for a guest with a confirmed reservation it is likely to lose the custom of that guest forever unless the situation is handled expertly.

Overbooking might also happen by accident – a mistake is made at some stage in the reservation process.

General procedure
The first step is to check whether the hotel really is full.

- Examine the housekeeper's report to see if there are any vacant rooms that are not shown on the room board or computer.
- Have any guests booked out during the day even though their reservation was for a longer stay?
- Is there anyone who should have booked out, but has not done so? The person may be intending to stay but has not bothered to check that it is possible. Or the person may have left without paying – but at least the room is available.
- Are there any rooms that have been taken out of service, for example for re-decoration, which could be put back into use, and let, if necessary at a reduced tariff?
- Are there any bookings that have not been confirmed? Can these be released or the customers contacted by phone?
- Are there any rooms let to staff which could be used for a guest that night? The staff could be booked into other accommodation.
- Have any cancellations been made during the day? The room records may not have been amended.
- Are there any bookings for two rooms which may be condensed into one by using extra beds? A family may be quite happy for four children to sleep in the same room, especially if this is less expensive. A tour operator may be prepared to ask members of the group to share rooms.
- Are there any confirmed bookings that can be released if the guests have not arrived by a certain time?
- Are there any guests shown as due to arrive when they have in fact arrived? If there are this will reduce the number of rooms still required.
- Are there any bookings which you suspect for one reason or another will turn out to be no shows?
- Is the arrival list correct? For example it might include a booking for the next day or a different month by mistake.
- Are there any rooms in the hotel, for example the sitting room of a suite, which can be converted into bedrooms?

Many hotels establish a daily routine of contacting hotel booking centres, tourist information offices and even other hotels in the area letting them know if they have accommodation available for the coming night. Hotels which appear to be in direct competition with each other may have a good working relationship and regularly help out each other by passing on bookings if they are full, or taking a guest that has been overbooked

---

✳ FOR INTEREST

A survey in the USA asked travellers what the most important factor was in their decision to return to a hotel:

	%
cleanliness/appearance	63
good service	42
price	39
facilities	35
convenience/location	32
quiet and private	9

Badly handled overbooking scored highly in the reasons for not returning.

The next step is to make the best of what is obviously going to be a difficult situation. First establish any priorities.

- Are there any VIPs due to arrive? These guests must get a room.
- Are there any other guests expected, for example regulars, who have priority?
- Find out if there are any bookings that correspond with the period the hotel is overbooked for. For example if the hotel is overbooked for the next two nights, it may be appropriate to book out a guest who has booked for two nights. This will reduce the total number of guests that have to be booked out.
- Avoid booking the same guest out more than once. Check guest history cards before deciding who to book out.
- Book out those who will do least damage to future business, for example a booking from a travel agent who rarely uses the hotel, or a guest from Europe who is on a touring holiday.
- Book out the least profitable business, for example customers on a bargain break.

If a guest with a confirmed reservation has to be booked into another hotel, the original hotel will be liable for any extra expenses incurred as a result of the change. For instance:

- taxi fares to the other hotel and from that hotel back to a business meeting set up in the original hotel
- costs of telephone calls to tell business colleagues of the change of venue for a breakfast meeting
- higher room charges because the replacement hotel is more expensive than the price originally confirmed to the guest.

Explaining to the guest

If a guest has to be booked into another hotel, apologise and explain the problem as tactfully and honestly as possible. If the guest gets angry do not interrupt but let the guest finish speaking then once again apologise. In many establishments it is the policy for the manager or a senior member of staff to be called if a guest has to be booked out. This will at least make the guest feel that he or she is important after all and that it was just a mistake by the staff.

Waitlisting customers

If a customer requests a booking and the establishment is full, the receptionist should offer to put the customer on the waiting list to be contacted if a cancellation is received. The receptionist might also suggest another hotel in the area, particularly if there is one belonging to the same consortium or company, or give the customer the telephone number of the local tourist information office which has details of other accommodation.

▶ ▶ ▶ TO DO

Prepare a room availability chart for an establishment of your choice for a seven day period. For each room type state the overbooking allowance. Then complete the chart to show that some rooms are overbooked on some of the days.

Alternatively

Contact the front office staff of three or four hotels in your area and ask them what factors they take into account before deliberately overbooking. Can they pass on any tips on how to deal with a guest who has to be booked out to another hotel?

XI Data Systems   THE XITEL DEMONSTRATION HOTEL   02NOV'

FORWARD   ROOMTYPE   AVAILABILITY

NOV 89	2 Thu	3 Fri	4 Sat	5 Sun	6 Mon	7 Tue	8 Wed	9 Thu	10 Fri	11 Sat	12 Sun	13 Mon	14 Tue	15 Wed	16 Thu	17 Fri	18 Sat	19 Sun	20 Mon	21 Tue	22 Wed	23 Thu	24 Fri	25 Sat	26 Sun	27 Mon	28 Tue	29 Wed	30 Thu
DOUBLE 553	19	14	15	15	15	15	20	20	20	20	20	20	20	20	20	20	20	20	20	20	20	20	20	20	20	20	20	20	20
EXECDBL 577	19	19	19	20	20	20	20	20	20	20	20	20	20	20	20	20	20	20	20	20	20	20	20	20	20	20	20	20	20
SINGLE 323	3	7	7	8	11	11	12	12	12	12	12	12	12	12	12	12	12	12	12	12	12	12	12	12	12	12	12	12	12
SUITE 173	5	6	6	6	6	6	6	6	6	6	6	6	6	6	6	6	6	6	6	6	6	6	6	6	6	6	6	6	6
TWIN 852	27	27	27	27	30	30	30	30	30	30	30	30	30	30	30	30	30	30	30	30	30	30	30	30	30	30	30	27	27
TOTAL 2478	73	73	74	76	82	82	88	88	88	88	88	88	88	88	88	88	88	88	88	88	88	88	88	88	88	88	88	85	85

Customers may start arriving very early on the day of their reservation, or in large numbers at one time so prepare as much as possible in advance.

1. All correspondence relating to each of the day's reservations should be carefully checked to ensure that the details have been recorded correctly.
   * Has the reservation been recorded for the correct date, the correct number of people and in the correct name?
   * Have any special requests been noted, for example for a non-smoking room or a room with wheelchair access?
   * Are the facilities booked what the guest requested/were confirmed as available?
   * Is there a history card for the customer? This may indicate that the person always expects a room with a minibar and video, or a special pillow, or is hard of hearing and requires a room with a suitable fire alarm. If the guest has complained on a previous visit a special room may be appropriate (the last one was apparently very noisy), or staff can be warned (room service was slow, there were no towels in the room). The history card might also warn staff of a guest who frequently causes trouble.
   * Has the method of payment been established?
   * Has the guest paid a deposit in advance? The cashier should be reminded that the deposit has to be credited to the guest's bill.
   * Is advance authorisation necessary, for example clearance from the customer's bank if payment will be made by cheque? If a company will be paying, does it have an account with the hotel? Have there been any difficulties in getting payment in the past?
   * What is the expected time of arrival?
2. Pass on details of the day's reservations to appropriate departments, drawing attention to special requests, for example for a cot to be placed in a room.
3. File correspondence relating to the day's reservations in an easily accessible place. Then if there is a particular query when a customer checks in, the details can be quickly checked.
4. Prepare the key cards, completing as many of the details as possible: guest name, room tariff, room number, date of arrival and date of departure (see unit 13). The cards can then be kept:
   * in a pigeon hole, perhaps with the room key and any messages waiting for the guest
   * in a filing box in alphabetical order by guest name, or numerical order by room number.
5. If electronic keys are used, these are sometimes prepared in advance and kept with the key card (see unit 23).
6. Complete the registration card as far as possible. For a regular guest, for example, it will be possible to complete all or most of the details so the guest has simply to sign the card on arrival. If this is done it is important to ask the person to check the form as some of the information may have changed, for example the guest has a new car, or there may be two guests with the same name and the details may be for the wrong one. (See unit 13.)
7. Sort out any mail or messages which have arrived in advance (these may have been filed in a bring forward system, for example) and put them with

Use a highlighter pen to draw attention to significant details or special requests on correspondence, arrival lists and similar documents

USEFUL TERMS

Release time   When the room may be put up for resale if the customer has not arrived. The time will vary according to the type of establishment, for example for hotels which have a lot of business people staying it may generally be 6 p.m., but if the person indicates an earlier arrival time, say 2 p.m., it may be three hours after that time. Customers should be informed of the release time when the booking is made.

Day let   A room let for all or part of the day (but not overnight). For instance for a small business meeting, or for airline crew who will be sleeping during the day in preparation for a long flight overnight. The room can usually be re-let for the night.

The information in this unit will help you gain the Caterbase module *Preparing for Arrivals*.

the key card or where they can be quickly found. If an important message is waiting a note might also be made next to the customer's name on the arrival list.

8. Prepare any information pack which should be handed to customers when they arrive, for example explaining arrangements for the conference or promoting a new facility in the hotel or town.

9. Allocate parking spaces. For example if a party of customers will be arriving by coach or minibus it may be necessary to organise a parking space for them late the previous evening so that it is easy to offload the luggage and get it into the establishment. Car parking spaces may have to be booked if space is limited or a special request has been made. Some establishments do not have their own car park but instead use one nearby, possibly by special arrangement, so in return for a fee the car park owners allow the establishment's customers to park free. In some establishments staff (the link man) will offer to park customers' cars for them.

Allocating rooms

The contents of mail and messages are important to the recipient, so there should never be any delay in passing them on, nor any risk of passing them to the wrong person (who may be dishonest and take advantage of the information)

Whatever system is used (see unit 11) it should take account of customer's expectations and the efficiency and profitability of the establishment.

1. Depending on establishment procedure, rooms may be allocated:
   * when the guest makes the booking and details are entered on the chart or in the computer
   * on the day itself (or the previous evening) when key cards and registration forms for all arrivals are prepared
   * at the time the guest registers.
2. Take account as far as possible of requests for specific rooms or the preferences of a regular customer (these should be available from the guest history card).
3. Avoid the need to move guests later if, for example, they are staying for several days.
4. Match check-out times to arrival times. For example if a guest is known to be checking out early, say the bill has been paid the previous evening, that room can be allocated to someone who will be checking in early.
5. Follow any establishment procedure for allocating rooms, for example: the nicest rooms in a particular category first, one floor or wing of the building at a time.

 GUESTCRAFT TIP

If a guest is checked into a room that has had extras put in there by mistake, such as flowers or a bottle of wine intended for a VIP, do not remove them. To do so might embarrass the guest. It will certainly be disappointing after the initial surprise and pleasure and the guest might never forget the error.

Make sure the VIP guest gets a replacement. If the VIP has already gone to the room it may be necessary to send a different extra so the guest is not aware a mistake has been made. For example if the VIP is a regular guest and always finds flowers in the room, then a tray of fresh canapes might be sent with a bottle of chilled wine and a personal note from the manager.

◆ ◆ ◆ **TO DO**

Make brief notes on what you would do if you had to deal with two of the following situations as a receptionist. Discuss your ideas with one or two people who have had experience of dealing with similar situations, note the additional points they make and with their help draw up a checklist which would reduce the chance of similar mistakes happening in the future.

A. Miss Hilda Warrington-Smith checks in stating that she has a guaranteed reservation. You can find no record of the booking, however a suitable room is available.

B. Mrs Mazzawi and her elderly mother check in. You find their reservation is for a double room. They do not speak very good English and you think they must have expected a double room to have two beds in it. All the twin rooms have already been allocated.

C. Mr Wylie arrives with a reservation which has been made and apparently confirmed by his travel agent. You find the booking (which is for three nights) entered in the hotel records for the next month. It is not immediately clear whose fault this was and the hotel is fully booked.

General procedure

1. Greet the person. A smile should be the first thing the customer receives from the receptionist, a smile which says 'We're glad to see you ... you have come to the right place ... I am here to help you.' (See units 5 and 25.)

2. Ask the person's name, then find the details of the booking. Confirm this with the customer, 'A twin room with bath Mrs Patel, for two nights and you have a travel agent's voucher for the accommodation charge.'

3. Ask the person to register. Provide help as necessary, for example the loan of a pen. Some guests may appreciate help in completing the form, particularly if they do not understand English well. Guests in wheelchairs should be taken to a table where they can complete the form (some reservation desks have a special part of the counter which is lower than the rest). Quickly check the registration entry to ensure that all the details are correct (see unit 13).

4. Check the room is ready if one has been pre-allocated, or allocate an appropriate room (see unit 35).

5. Issue the person with a key and key card. In some establishments keys are kept at the porter's desk and handed over once customers have identified themselves, for example by providing a key card. (See units 13, 35 and 53.) If you think it appropriate, tactfully remind the customers of the check-out time by offering to put their luggage in store, for example.

6. Hand over any mail or messages.

7. According to establishment procedure, enquire if the person would like:
   - a table booked in the restaurant for dinner
   - an early morning wake-up call/tea/coffee/continental breakfast and if so at what time
   - a newspaper and if so which one.

8. Arrange for help with luggage and car parking.

9. Direct the person to the room. The receptionist may simply explain how the guest will find his/her room. Remember that some guests get lost quite easily, so instructions should be given slowly and clearly. Alternatively receptionist or porters may escort guests to their rooms, pointing out on the way various hotel facilities and explaining those in the room, such as the tea and coffee making equipment, radio and television.

10. As soon as possible after the guest has checked in, mark the arrivals list to indicate that the person has arrived and what room number he or she is in. Also up-date the room status system. Try and avoid any possibility of a colleague sending another guest to the same room (see unit 11).

11. Notify the appropriate departments that the person has arrived (see unit 15). Telephone calls for the guest can then be dealt with efficiently and quickly.

12. Open an account for the guest, entering details on the tabular ledger or into the computer (see unit 20).

Special procedures

- Full or part pre-payment may be required on arrival if, for example the booking was not confirmed (see unit 32).

When they first arrive in the establishment customers will make their way, or be directed to the reception desk to register. This is a process many customers wish to get over quickly, especially if they have had a long, tiring journey or a hard day at work

The information in units 36 and 27 will help you gain the Caterbase module *Dealing with Arrivals.*

‼ REMEMBER

- If the first impression a customer forms of an establishment is good that person will be more inclined to ignore minor irritations that may occur throughout the stay.
- An unattended reception desk is a security risk. It will also make an arriving customer who is not sure what to do feel uneasy.
- If you are busy when a customer arrives at the reception desk acknowledge the person with a smile and if possible a few words such as 'I will be with you in just a moment, madam.'
- If a person pays in full in advance in cash it is a good policy to ask (tactfully) for some means of identification. Cash customers are not as desirable as they might seem if they leave the hotel with equipment and other property from the room and possibly rob other guests.

- If a deposit has been paid in advance the customer's copy of the receipt should be checked to make sure the deposit has not been paid by another Mrs James, for example.
- In some hotels, guests paying by credit card are asked by the receptionist for their card on arrival. An imprint is taken and the guest asked to sign the otherwise blank voucher (see unit 46).
- If a person has to wait for some time, for example because the room is not ready, suggest somewhere pleasant he or she can wait. In these circumstances some hotels will offer a complimentary drink.

Late arrivals

Many hotels set a certain time limit on how long they will honour reservations for that day. Guests will usually be asked what time they expect to arrive when they make the booking. The reservations confirmation will note a late time of arrival, if known, but otherwise warn customers that the booking will only be held until 6 p.m., for example. After this time the room may be sold to anyone who requires it.

If a person with a reservation does not arrive and does not contact the hotel to cancel the arrangement, then a contract has to be broken. The hotel can claim compensation and keep any deposit which has been paid (see unit 50).

Guaranteed reservations will automatically be held until the following day if the customer fails to arrive. The hotel will then charge for the accommodation (but possibly not for the breakfast if it is an inclusive rate). Usually guaranteed reservations are only accepted when the hotel can easily recover the cost – for example the person booking will be asked for his or her credit card details or the person (or the person's company) has an account with the hotel.

If the reservation is for two or more days and the customer has not arrived after the first day, attempts will usually be made to find out what has gone wrong before the reservation is released.

If at the time the reservation is taken, such details as 'Requires late breakfast on arrival' are established and recorded, then the arrivals process will go smoothly for customers and for receptionists

◆ ◆ ◆ **TO DO**

Carry out a small survey among (honest) friends of yours. How many times have they or people they know booked a hotel room or restaurant table and not taken up the reservation or cancelled it in advance? How do they feel hotels and restaurants can overcome this sort of problem?

Showing guests to their room

- Use the person's name wherever appropriate.
- Be sensitive to the guest's needs. A lady who tells you she is attending a celebration dinner that evening might be pleased to know there is a hairdressing salon in the hotel – provided you don't seem to be suggesting she needs to have her hair done.
- Be sensitive to the guest's mood. Don't be too talkative if the guest seems very tired or answers questions as briefly as possibly.
- Avoid talking about politics, religion or football if there is a danger of making a controversial remark which upsets the guest. Talking about the weather may not be considered very interesting or imaginative by some guests either.
- Precede the guest into the room. You can quickly find the light switches and so forth because you know the layout of the room. Also if a mistake has been made and there is already someone in the room by entering the room first you can quickly assess the situation, reduce the level of embarrassment and offer apologies to those concerned. In some establishments staff showing guests to their rooms always knock on the door first – but the guest may think (quite understandably) that this should never be necessary.
- If the room is too hot or too cold offer to adjust the heating or air-conditioning and open or shut the windows as appropriate. If it is dark outside when a guest is shown to the room offer to draw the curtains.
- Never appear to be soliciting for a tip/gratuity.

Take reservations		XI-TEL Demonstration		RETAK A,Ø1 Ø1JAN92	
1. Contact		MR ANDREW ADAMS]		Folio	1Ø
2. Arrival......		[Ø JAN 92] Time......[12ØØ]		Taken by	
3. Departure...		[Ø5 JAN 92] Nights [4]		Date...[Ø1 JAN 92]	
4. Plan Details		Nightly single room rate		Single room	
Plancode		Rate Roomtype Rooms		Sleepers Alloc	
[RACKSING]		[44.7Ø] [SINGLE] [1]		[1] [N]	
[ ]		[ ] [ ] [ ]		[ ] [ ]	
5. Guest Data		Groupname			
Surname		Title		Initials	
BONNER					
6. Payment Details		Deposit		Folio	
		Ø.ØØ		Plan	1Ø
		Ø.ØØ		Normal	1Ø
7. Statistic Data				Extra	1Ø
Business source		INTASUN Rating code		MEDIUM	1Ø
8. Folio Remarks					
	Requires late breakfast on arrival				
	Short staffed due to New Year holiday				[+]
	Selected field [1]				
F1 Help	F3 Exit prog	F8 Accept	F9 Comments	F10 Enquiry	F12 Cancel

Guests who have not booked

Sometimes people arrive at a hotel on the chance that they will find accommodation for themselves. They have not made a reservation, perhaps because their journey plans have suddenly changed. Most hotels welcome these 'chance arrivals' as they are known.

1. Find out the type of room, number of people in party and length of stay required.
2. Check the availability. If the exact requirement is not available offer alternatives. Allocate the accommodation.
3. Ask the guest to register.
4. If pre-payment or a deposit is required work out the amount due, say the price of the room multiplied by the number of nights the guest wishes to stay plus the cost of any extras which are required such as breakfast.
5. Complete a key card and give it and a key to the guest.
6. Point out the restaurants, bar and so forth and direct the guest to the room.

Guests who have not confirmed

Unconfirmed reservations offer the establishment little security, so many hotels ask for a deposit or full prepayment in these circumstances. Of course if the guest is a regular customer, there will be no need for this precaution or any special procedure.

Handling guest's luggage

- Check carefully with the guest what luggage needs carrying. This will ensure that nothing is left behind.
- Do not allow any luggage to be left unattended in case of theft.
- Take special care of fragile items.
- Report any suspicious items.
- If luggage has to be stored, do not stack it too high otherwise it might cause an accident or the luggage could be damaged.
- Do not put luggage which has got wet in the rain straight on to the carpet of the foyer or room.
- Use a lift when transferring heavy luggage if possible, not the stairs.
- Hang up suits, overcoats and similar items carried loose or in a carrying bag on a hanger.
- Place suitcases on the special racks in the room (if provided) or where they will be convenient for the guests and not cause a tripping hazard.
- Show respect for hotel furnishings and guests' luggage.
- Do not release luggage from storage without the correct luggage receipt pass being produced or suitable confirmation that it belongs to the claimant.

Undesirable guests

Potential guests should never be allowed to suspect that they are on a black list, as this would lead to legal difficulties (see units 16 and 49).

- Become familiar with the names on the black list by referring to it regularly at a time of the day when there are no guests about, or by doing so out of sight of guests.
- If it is necessary to check the black list when there are guests at the reception desk pretend it is an ordinary document, for example a diary or arrivals list, and examine it away from any guest.
- The excuse that the hotel is full may not always convince a person on the black list, so if you are in difficulty summon the help of a manager quickly.

This information and the information in unit 43 will help you gain the Caterbase module *Handling Guest Luggage.*

Group arrivals

Special procedures are called for when groups of ten or more people are due to arrive at the same time.

- It may be more convenient to set up a separate reception area for the use of the group alone so that other guests wishing to check in are not delayed or inconvenienced. A function room may be useful for this purpose, or if the hotel is very large and does a lot of tour business it may have a separate purpose-built reception area.
- Prepare as much as possible in advance. For example an envelope containing a completed key card and room key can be prepared ready to hand to each guest as soon as he or she has registered. An information pack can also be given to the guest at this point.
- Try and give all members of the group paying the same price the same type of room. If one member of the group has a higher standard of room than the others this may lead to dissatisfaction among the rest of the group.
- Use the arrivals or rooming list to check off the names of group members as they collect their keys and register.
- Watch out for last minute substitutions of group members and change the details as necessary, passing on the new information to the telephonist and other departments which need to know the names of tour members.
- Set aside an area for the group's luggage while the guests are checking in or arrange for it to be left in the coach until it can be carried direct to the bedrooms.

‼ REMEMBER

A guest's luggage can indicate much about the person. An observant receptionist may be able to notice the tell-tale signs of a dishonest guest.

- Very light, but large suitcase: the person may be planning to fill it with property stolen from the hotel and other guests.
- Very little luggage when the guest has booked for several nights: the person may be intending to leave without paying.

Never put keys in bedroom doors ready for group arrivals. While this practice may seem convenient for the guests and staff, it will give the professional hotel thief as well as the opportunist thief a wonderful opportunity:

- to remove contents from rooms
- to make copies of keys so that they can return as often as they like to steal the guests' belongings.

?? HOW TO

Handle heavy luggage

- Take special care as the weight of the suitcase may not be obvious.
- Do not risk injury by carrying too many cases at once.
- Be careful not to knock into others while carrying cases in and out of lifts and around corners.
- When bulky or very large objects require moving it is usually safer to use a trolley or hand truck.

Carrying by hand

- Pick up the suitcase slowly and smoothly, not with a jerk which can cause a strain.
- Bend at the knees until the hand, with an extended arm, reaches the handle of the case.

Using a trolley

- Do not overload the trolley and make sure it is not stacked so high that there is no longer a clear view ahead.
- When stacking the trolley, place larger, heavier items at the bottom so that the trolley is stable and smaller items are not crushed.
- When pushing a trolley avoid damaging back muscles by keeping the:
  - back straight
  - arms out-stretched in front against the trolley handle
  - chin tucked in
  - body tilting forward so that the rear leg, back and back of the head are in a straight line.
- Pull trolleys through doorways rather than pushing them, ensuring that the coast is clear.

 TO DO

Take two aspects of dealing with group arrivals, for example registration and handling the luggage, and consider what steps can be taken to speed up the procedure in a typical hotel such as arranging with the tour organiser for the guests to:

- complete their registration forms on the coach before they arrive and for the courier to collect the forms
- clearly mark each piece of luggage with their name so the porters know what room to take it to from the arrivals list.

If you can, get help from staff who are used to dealing with large groups.

Receptionists are right if they believe that the customer expects them to know everything:
- the time of the last train
- the soup of the day
- whether Mrs Armstrong is a guest
- the exact whereabouts of the crèche organiser.

Of course you cannot know everything, but it should be within your power to satisfy the customer's need, whatever the nature of the enquiry. You should have:
- a list of all the facilities, services and products your establishment sells, with details such as price and opening times
- a knowledge of the rules and policies of your establishment and of the law as regards your workplace, for instance, young people under 18 cannot buy alcoholic drinks from the bar, or radios and cassette recorders are not allowed at the poolside
- a list of names of members of staff, their telephone extension numbers if relevant, and their job titles
- knowledge of what is happening from day to day throughout the establishment, together with the names and contact numbers of the people (customers and staff) involved
- a good idea of what goes on in the locality so that you can inform guests looking for details of church services, entertainment, the post office, the library and so on
- good reference sources to hand, such as local papers (for entertainment, shops, emergency service numbers), telephone directories, the *Yellow Pages* or the *Thompson Directory* and *Kelly's Business Directory*, relevant street maps, a copy of *Who's Who*.

You should also know what enquiries it is better not to try and answer yourself but to pass on to the appropriate person. For example:
- what special discounts can be given to a group booking – the front office manager or another senior manager
- whether the hotel has facilities for a wedding party for 200 – the banqueting manager or sales manager
- if the hairdresser or masseur can come to the guest's room – the manager of the department concerned
- can the receptionist book an airline seat or make a train reservation – a local travel agent
- whether an urgent report can be typed by the receptionist – a local secretarial service (or the hotel may have its own business bureau).

General procedure

- Greet the customer with a warm smile.
- Listen carefully to find out the requirements.
- Make a note of the relevant details if necessary.
- To avoid misunderstanding, repeat the main points back to the customer. Take special care if the enquiry is complicated, or the person has difficulty hearing.
- Ask further questions if you are still unsure, 'What type of food do you like?'

Know your job, know what others are responsible for, know the services and facilities on offer, know the rules, policies and legal obligations of your workplace

If you're not sure of the answer to an enquiry, don't guess. Look it up, or ask someone who does know

The information in this unit will help you gain the Caterbase module *Handling Enquiries*. It will also help you gain the module *Handling Mail and Keys* (see also units 23, 35, 36, 40, 53 and 58).

- Deal with the enquiry immediately.
- Offer the options: 'There are lots of restaurants near here, Sir.' 'Here are a few cards of the local restaurants, Sir ...'
- Recommend a course of action '...May I suggest that you try our restaurant on the first floor?'
- Offer to do the legwork 'I'll just check for you Sir.'
- Confirm what has been arranged between you, if applicable: 'That's a table for four at 8 p.m. this evening.'
- Finish the exchange on a positive note: 'I hope you enjoy your meal.'

Telephone enquiries

When dealing with queries over the phone never leave the enquirer hanging on. If the request takes time to sort out explain at each stage what you intend to do, for instance, 'I understand that the crèche is normally for children under eight, but I will check with the organiser to see whether she can make an exception in Bobby's case. I won't keep you a moment, Mrs Sutra.'

Another example

Good morning sir, can I help you?
Good morning. I wonder if you can tell me where the nearest good restaurant is?
There are several restaurants near here sir, what type of food do you like?
French or Italian mainly.
Here are a few cards of the local restaurants sir, but I suggest you try our restaurant on the first floor. It has a classical French menu and there are one or two Chef's specials every day.
What is the speciality for today?
Sole Véronique, fillets of lemon sole in a white wine sauce garnished with grapes, and carbonnade de boeuf, a tender stew with beer as the main ingredient. Would you like to see the menu, sir?
Yes please. Are there tables for tonight?
I'll just check for you sir, I won't keep you a moment.
Yes, there are sir, would you like me to reserve a table?
Yes please for two at 8 p.m.
And the name sir?
Ridgeley
Thank you Mr Ridgeley. That's a table for two people at 8 p.m. this evening. I hope you enjoy your meal.
Thank you for your help.
You're most welcome, goodbye.

▶▶▶ TO DO

Libraries are a good source of information. The larger public libraries and those attached to colleges and workplaces in the hotel, catering, leisure and tourism area have specialist books, periodicals and bibliographies (list of relevant books). Visit a good library and find out how the index systems work. It may be an idea to have a particular project or topic in mind for which you need information.

Alternatively
Ask the receptionists at two or three establishments of your choice to tell you about the kind of enquiries they have received. What are the most common types? Are there any queries which were difficult and how did the receptionist deal with them? Think about whether the receptionists could have handled the difficult enquiries in a way which satisfied the customers' needs more effectively and how? How did the receptionists handle *your* enquiries?

The best way to deal with a complaint is to prevent it from occurring.
1. Listen to what the customers are asking for.
2. Watch what people are doing. Learn how to read body language so that you can judge what people are thinking and feeling, and anticipate their needs.
3. Take messages effectively.
4. Attend promptly to customers' needs.

But even in the best run establishments things can go wrong, and customers can become very dissatisfied. Situations which might lead to a complaint from a customer are:

where a member of staff has
failed to do something properly
misunderstood the customer
forgotten to do something
forgotten to pass on a message

where the customer
has been kept waiting
expects something which
 is not usually provided
feels that he or she is
 not getting value for money

and where
equipment or supplies are broken, damaged or missing.

See *Customercraft* video and book.

General procedure

- Listen to the complaint until the customer has finished speaking. Do not interrupt.
- Apologise but do not admit that you or the establishment are to blame.
- Do not make excuses or blame anyone else, especially the customer.
- Never argue, disagree or become aggressive.
- Keep calm and remain polite.
- Try to put the problem right yourself. If you cannot, get help from your supervisor or manager.
- Never offer something the establishment cannot provide.
- Thank the customer for bringing the matter to your attention.
- Check afterwards that the customer is satisfied with the action taken.
- Record the complaint according to the policies of your establishment, and make sure your supervisor knows.

'Awkward' customers

There is no such thing as an awkward customer, though if you listen to staff you might think so-called awkward customers are the main source of frustration, mirth or just plain tedium. All customers are important, no matter what

Always try and put yourself in the customer's shoes when dealing with his or her complaint. Ask yourself how you would like to be treated in the same circumstances

the reason is that makes them demanding. They may have had a row at home, a bad day at work, a splitting headache, just missed their train, or a hundred and one other reasons. Think of the times when you have not felt your best.

As a receptionist there is a lot you can do to satisfy an 'awkward' customer. Try to see the situation as a challenge to your skills in dealing with customers rather than as a tiresome problem. Avoid the temptation to react in the same way as the customer. Customers can be:

Rude Keep calm, don't get involved, and don't take the customer's anger personally.

Sarcastic 'This is not what I would call a *bona fide* Swedish sauna, but then I don't expect you would know one anyway.' Don't be intimidated, don't put customers down. Do flatter customers and know what your establishment can offer so that you can answer their questions. Remain polite.

Over-demanding 'I want your best bridal suite. If someone else is using it you must ask them to move to another room.' Explain to the customer what you can and cannot do. Offer an alternative.

Angry 'In all my years as a patron of this establishment I have never had such disgusting treatment!' Keep calm, don't argue, apologise and take action immediately to put things right.

Violent 'I'll rearrange your face!' Keep calm, never tackle the person yourself, but call your manager or supervisor immediately.

Customers with special needs

Avoid complaints from customers with special needs. Try to anticipate the requirements of children, the elderly and the handicapped. It is important to know whether your establishment has facilities to meet their needs. If you are unsure what the customer wants, then do not be afraid to ask. And without fussing remain aware of their needs throughout their visit.

Handling compliments

It is surprising how difficult it is for some people to handle a compliment. One reaction is to laugh it off or belittle what you are being complimented about which is bound to put off the person giving the compliment. Thank the customer politely, with a smile, 'How nice of you to say so. Thank you.' If the compliment is for someone else make sure the person knows it will be passed on.

 GUESTCRAFT TIP

If possible take the person with the complaint to another room or more private area. It is never a good idea for other customers to hear other people's complaints because they may lose confidence in the establishment.

Customers do not enjoy making a complaint. And between 65% and 95% of dissatisfied customers who do not complain will not visit your establishment again. Up to 95% of dissatisfied customers who do complain will become loyal customers if their complaints are handled well and quickly. So think of customers who complain as doing your establishment a favour. All you have to do then is to make sure that by the time the customer leaves the premises he or she is fully satisfied.

Courtesy to the disabled

- Be careful not to treat disabled people differently when it is not necessary to do so, for example by speaking to a disabled adult as if he or she is a child.
- Avoid leaning or hanging on to a person's wheelchair. By doing so you are invading the person's body space and this will be annoying.
- If you are talking to a person in a wheelchair for more than a few minutes pull up a chair and sit down so you are on the same level, otherwise you are both likely to develop a stiff neck.
- Do not assume that people in wheelchairs want to be pushed. Some can wheel themselves around expertly.
- If you do help move a person in a wheelchair, do not leave him or her unattended in a dangerous place, for example in a busy doorway or on a steep slope.
- If a person cannot see at all, or very poorly, always identify yourself and anyone with you (explaining for example that your companion is on your left).
- If a person has difficulty hearing do speak slowly, clearly and expressively. If you then realise or know already that the person can lip read always look directly at the person when you are talking. Keep hands, food and cigarettes away from your mouth. Avoid standing with your back to a window or bright light which makes it difficult for the person to see your face. Be prepared to write notes if a particular part of the conversation is difficult to get across.
- If the person has difficulty speaking be patient and encouraging. Avoid correcting the person or trying to take over what the person is saying. When necessary ask short questions that can be quickly answered, or only require a nod of the head or other gesture. Do not pretend to understand something that you don't. If necessary repeat what you do understand checking from the person's reactions whether or not you are right.

 TO DO

Ask some receptionists what most complaints from customers are about, and what they do to resolve these problems. Then practise handling some of the situations with a colleague or friend. One of you plays the customer the other the receptionist. Then swap roles. Afterwards discuss how the 'customer' felt.

A receptionist could almost be described as the messenger of the establishment, except that he or she would not normally be physically rushing from A to B making sure that the right person received the message. Technology has seen to that. Messages can be received and sent by:

- telephone (see unit 27 and 59)
- in person (see unit 26)
- mail (see unit 28 and 58)
- fax and telex (see unit 29)
- train, car or motor-bike
- another person.

Messages are normally conveyed either in writing or verbally. Many will need to be passed on by the receptionist to another person who may be:

- a member of staff
- a customer, guest, conference delegate, visitor
- friend, relative or colleague of a customer
- a potential customer.

If you receive a message for someone else verbally it is always a good idea to write it down rather than pass it on verbally yourself, especially if the message is complicated or the person to receive it is not available straight away.

Good receptionists know that a large part of their job is taking messages and always making sure they have message pad and pen to hand

written messages	*verbal messages*
are permanent	may never be passed on
are more likely to be accurate	may get distorted in the telling
help make sure you don't forget the details	may miss out important facts
can be referred to later	are difficult to check for accuracy.

The switchboard operator is often in the first line of fire when a caller has a complaint or is upset, regardless of whose fault it may be. It takes a lot of skill and patience to calm callers once aroused. One way of avoiding an awkward situation arising is to make sure that you do your job effectively by:

- keeping calls short
- asking callers to repeat themselves if you have not understood
- double checking the facts by repeating them to the caller
- repeating any numbers and spellings
- repeating any messages back to the caller in full.

See unit 27.

Taking messages

1. Establish who the message is for.
2. Write down a message accurately with all the relevant details:
   - think what the recipient needs to know
   - be concise
   - make sure the facts are correct.

   The most common mistakes when taking down messages over the phone are:
   - missing out a figure from a telephone number
   - forgetting to ask the caller's name
   - forgetting to take the caller's telephone number.
3. Repeat the message back to the caller.
4. Pass on the message immediately, or as soon as possible.
5. Check if possible that the recipient has understood.

Technology can help ensure messages are accurate, legible and reach the correct person without delay. This message printing machine is linked to flashing message-waiting lights in the bedrooms

---

  TO DO

You get the message opposite. It does not tell you what action you should take. In fact it is about as much use as getting no message at all, except that it does warn you that there is probably trouble in store.

Quickly getting over your anger, you reflect that an urgent message which you cannot follow up means that you are probably not the only one let down by the person who took the message. You decide positive action will be better than a telling off.

Step one
Make a poster to help remind everyone what a good message should look like. Label your sample message to identify the key points it should cover.
1. Day and time of message.
2. Name of the caller and his or her company. Check you have got it right by repeating it to the caller.
3. Reason for calling.
4. Phone number for a return call (or the address), and details of when the caller is available.
5. Your name and job title or department/section.

Step two
Invent a horrific series of events which could happen in a hotel, catering, leisure or tourism establishment after the receptionist fails to pass on a message effectively either from or to a customer. The end result should be that the customer threatens to sue the establishment. Try to keep the sequence of events – what happens and what is said – within the realms of possibility. Truth is stranger (more horrific) than fiction!

Test out your scenario by describing it to colleagues. Then with their help make any amendments which would improve its effectiveness when used as part of a training session and note:
- what mistakes were made
- the precise points at which they were made.

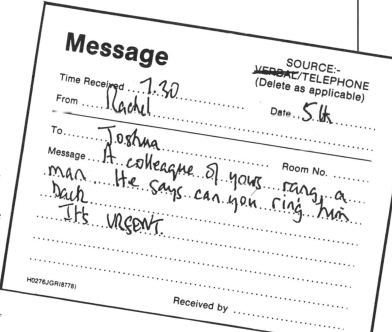

Message

SOURCE:-
VERBAL/TELEPHONE
(Delete as applicable)

Time Received ....7.30....

From ......Rachel......

Date...5.k..

To........Joshua........

Room No. ......

Message....A colleague of yours.. rang. a
man. He says can you ring him
back
It's URGENT.

H0276JGR(8778)

Received by ......

An efficient system for dealing with guest bills will ensure that:
- all charges which the guest is liable to pay are paid
- the bill can be produced quickly when the guest is ready to pay it or is asked to pay it
- the establishment knows at particular points in time how much guests are due to pay and if guests have arrived in advance, what amounts have been paid and by whom
- mistakes are avoided, for example charging the wrong guest or charging the same guest twice for a particular item.

When exactly a bill is opened varies according to the system in use and establishment procedures.

In advance of the guest's arrival This means that the work can be fitted into a quiet moment, for example in the afternoon. The disadvantage is that if the guest does not arrive the work may be wasted. Bills will still have to be opened for those guests who arrive without an advance booking.

On arrival Opening the guest bill then becomes part of the arrivals procedure. With computer systems the bill is effectively opened the moment the computer is told the guest has arrived. It may not be printed out until the guest asks to settle the account.

When the first charge is received This can work well when the only charges to go on the bill come from other documents – meal or drink checks for example. Where certain charges, for example overnight accommodation in a hotel, are not backed by a voucher but added to bills as part of a systematic process, it can be confusing when a check has to be made for each room to see if a bill has already been opened.

When the guest is due to pay This is the system used in many restaurants and it works well when the bills are simple to prepare, involving one or at the most three or four checks giving the details of what has to be charged. It also works in a guesthouse or small hotel where the charges to guests are easy to work out and fairly standard.

General procedure

1. A bill should be opened in the name of each person due at some stage to pay money. In a hotel or guesthouse this usually means one bill per room, but in some instances if a number of rooms and guests are being paid for by one person all the charges will be put to a bill in that person's name.
2. The room number(s) and name(s) concerned should be written on the bill (computers will usually do this automatically).
3. Any standard charges, such as the cost of overnight accommodation, are added to all the bills at a particular time. This may be on arrival for new guests and in the afternoon for guests staying on, last thing at night or first thing in the morning. A systematic procedure for posting accommodation charges for each additional night's stay will reduce the chance of overlooking some guests.
4. Special procedures are followed for guests who pay by the week or month, a situation that might occur in a resort hotel or a student hall of residence. For example if the charge is paid in advance the bill may be made up and presented for payment a few days before the period begins.

> **!! REMEMBER**
>
> Certain guests may not be allowed to charge items to their bill. For example delegates on a conference or members of an inclusive tour may be required by the organiser or tour operator to pay cash for any extra at the time it is taken. In other instances such guests may be allowed to charge extras to their bill on the understanding they settle up before they leave.

5. Charges for any items that are not included in the accommodation tariff must be added or posted to guest bills separately. In a self-catering leisure centre, for example, where visitors can charge meals taken in the restaurant to their bill, the details are sent to the front office at the end of meal service, when they might be added to guest bills immediately or kept for a convenient moment. Special care has to be taken in hotels which charge separately for breakfast – the details must be added to the bill very quickly otherwise there is a chance the guest may already have settled the bill and left the hotel.

6. Guests who wish to have items added to their bill rather than pay for them at the time are asked to sign a charge voucher. Then if there is any query over the charge the original document can be checked. (See unit 44.)

7. Whatever system is used for guest billing, the procedure for adding charges includes four essential steps:
   - identifying the bill the charge should be added to (usually done by room number)
   - entering the amount of the charge
   - entering enough details for the guest to be able to tell what the charge is for and providing this information in such a way that the establishment can calculate the total charges made over a period of time for particular departments or types of product (for example room service or the restaurant)
   - signifying clearly on any charge vouchers that the amount has been added to the guest's bill (to prevent the charge being added again).

8. Computers will automatically update the total of each guest bill when a new charge is added. The appropriate function on the computer is selected, such as 'add charges' and the operator then follows the instructions on the screen.

9. Hotel billing machines (still used by a few hotels) hold the details of the previous balance in their memory. With the less sophisticated billing machines the previous total has to be picked up (in other words entered) after the room number has been keyed in. The new bill total is calculated automatically.

10. If a manual billing system is used, such as the tabular ledger (see unit 18), the charge is written in the appropriate column, for example bars, and against the appropriate room number. The total will not be calculated until the guest is due to pay and is unlikely to be incurring further charges.

11. With some machines the operator places the charge voucher in a special slot on the machine for it to be overprinted with the details that have been entered on the bill: date, room number, amount of charge and nature of charge.

12. Once the bills have been opened and until they are finally settled, they are kept in a suitable filing system:
    - in the computer's memory
    - in a special bill tray or drawer, with divisions for each room.

13. Once vouchers have been processed they are also filed:
    - with the bill
    - in a special voucher tray with divisions for each room
    - in pigeon holes.

Deposits and part-payment
If a deposit is being held for a guest the amount should be credited to the guest's bill when the bill is first opened.

If guests ask to pay their bill at regular intervals during their stay, the payment is credited and the bill returned to the bill tray (or kept open in the computer). Many establishments have a policy of requesting part payment the moment a bill reaches a specific limit. This reduces the danger of bad debts.

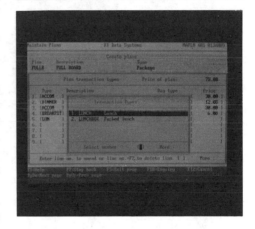

Many computer systems allow charges to be added to guest bills from terminals in the restaurant, bar, leisure centre and so forth. The guest is still asked to sign a voucher and this is kept in case there is a query.

▶ ▶ ▶ **TO DO**

Compare the filing system for guest bills and vouchers in three hotels. Try and choose hotels which are as different as possible from each other in size, facilities and the sort of customers they attract. Write a brief report so that you can discuss with your tutor or supervisor the way each system works, its advantages and disadvantages.

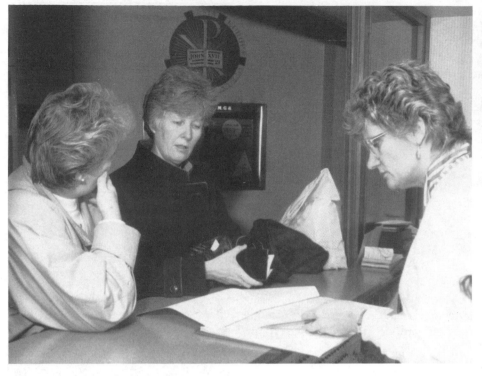

Guests are often in a hurry to check out and some get impatient when they have to wait in a queue or a long time is taken to produce their bill or answer queries. Careful preparation will reduce these problems. It will also reduce the risk of making mistakes which cost the establishment money, cause embarrassment and may result in the customer not returning and telling others about the inefficiency.

Advance preparation

1. Towards the end of each day the booking details for each guest should be checked to extract a list of everyone due to depart the following morning. This departure list (see unit 15) will also alert housekeeping, the restaurant and switchboard staff and anyone else who might supply guests with a service or facility at the last moment. The details can then be rushed to the front office and added to the bill before it is settled.
2. Before guests start departing a check should be made that all outstanding vouchers have been dealt with.
3. The method of payment should also be checked in advance. If the guest has already given a signature for the bill to be charged to a credit card, authorisation may be required from the credit card company (the likely amount of the bill will be known at this stage).
4. Unless charges are likely to be incurred at the last moment, add up the bill to produce a total. (This may even be done with computer systems, especially if the printer tends to be slow, or there are not enough printers to cope with busy periods.)

✱ FOR INTEREST

Experienced reception staff often have a good idea of the pattern of departures. Business people will usually leave quite early. Tourists may also leave early especially if they are travelling to their next hotel. On the other hand holidaymakers with their own car may prefer a more leisurely departure. There are various means of letting guests know the latest departure time – a statement on the key card or notice in each bedroom for example. Usually the departure time is a reasonable one for the sort of people using the establishment – 11 a.m. or 12 noon for resort and most tourist hotels, possibly quite early in the morning for youth hostels. If guests do want to stay a few hours extra the hotel may make a charge. Most establishments will be pleased to make arrangements to store guest luggage if they have finished with their room but are not leaving the locality until later in the day. (See unit 43.)

General procedure

1. Greet the guest (by name if possible) and ask for the room number of the bills which are to be paid (if the guest is well known there should be no need to ask for the room number).
2. Collect the bill from the bill tray and any vouchers which are attached to it. If a computer system is used, print out the bill.
3. Hand the bill to the guest with an appropriate and courteous remark: 'This is your bill, Miss World, for room 1006. The extra charges are all detailed and I have the vouchers supporting them if you would like me to check anything.' (See unit 44.)
4. Take the payment and give any change which is due (see units 44, 45 and 46) and a receipted bill.
5. Thank and say goodbye to the guest. 'Thank you for staying with us, Miss World. Everyone in Piddleton-on-Sea was thrilled when you were chosen Miss World and it's great you have found time to visit us. I do hope you have enjoyed your stay and that we will have the pleasure of seeing you again.'

    If the guest is likely to be visiting the area again in the near future, or is travelling to another area where other associated hotels are located, offer to make a reservation. (See units 9 and 10.)
6. File the copy of the paid bill and any vouchers which need to be kept in case of a future query.
7. Notify all the appropriate departments that the guest has:
    • departed
    • vacated the room
    • settled the bill but requires use of the room until ...
    • will be calling at ... to collect luggage left for safe-keeping.
8. Amend the front office records including the room status system to indicate that the guest has departed and the room will be ready for re-letting once housekeeping have cleaned and checked it.

USEFUL TERMS

Stay ons or **stop-overs** Alternative terms for *overstays* (see unit 32). Customers who continue their stay beyond their original departure date. **Extra departures** Alternative term for *understays* (see unit 32). Customers who leave before their original departure date.

‼ REMEMBER

Telephone calls received after a guest has left the establishment should be dealt with carefully for security reasons. The normal practice is simply to explain that the guest has already left. If it is an emergency the enquirer should be put through to a manager who can help.

Mail received after a guest has left should be re-addressed – to a forwarding address if one has been given, or to the address given on the booking confirmation or registration form. Details of mail forwarded in this way should be kept, for example in a mail forwarding book.

GUESTCRAFT TIP

When a hotel is expecting to be very busy the next day and there will be guests arriving early, or housekeeping are having difficulty in organising the room-cleaning schedule, receptionists might need to ask guests what time they intend leaving. This requires tact. Guests will not want to feel pressurised to leave early, but approached in the right way should understand why the hotel needs to know on this occasion.

Remember that not all guests want to check out in a hurry. People on holiday may not want to rush their departure as it signals the end of an enjoyable holiday and the prospect of returning to an overflowing in-tray in the office.

If a room has not been vacated by the check-out time and the guest cannot be contacted, the housekeeping staff may be able to help from their knowledge of the guest and how the guest has left the room on previous days (if the stay has been for a few days). It may look as though the guest is staying on (and had forgotten to inform reception), or there has been some problem (the guest may be ill in bed or been unable to return to the room to pack). It is also quite possible that all the guest's belongings (and perhaps some of the hotel's) have gone from the room and it must be assumed the guest has deliberately left without paying.

♦ ♦ ♦ TO DO

In most hotels there is a risk of certain charges being overlooked – because the voucher arrives at the front office after the guest has left and the guest has forgotten to mention anything about it. Discuss this problem with some of your colleagues and draw up a list of the charges which can be missed in this way and what can be done by the management and staff to improve the situation.

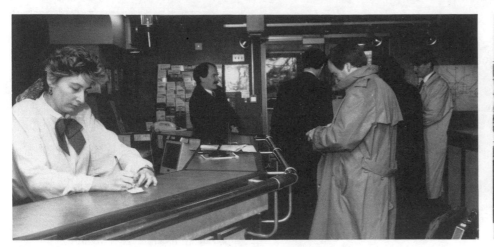

When housekeeping staff find guest property left behind in a room they will hand it to reception with details on where and when it was found. Regular inspections reduce the risk of lost property remaining some time before discovery, and increase the chance of establishing the owner

Luggage

Some people prefer to carry their own luggage when they depart, especially if they are travelling by car and do not have much to carry. Some people know they are staying in the sort of establishment where help with luggage is part of the service, and will ask for a porter. Other people are not able to carry their own luggage – there is too much or they are elderly, for example – and if porters are not available other front office or even housekeeping staff will have to help.

General procedure
1. Confirm the details of the person requiring assistance: name and room number, and indicate that a porter is on the way, or will be with the guest as soon as possible (give an estimated time).
2. The porter or member of staff sent to help should establish what needs to be carried, for example hanging suitcases to be collected from the cupboard. This will avoid items being left behind.
3. Check where the luggage has to be taken:
   • down to reception while the guest settles the bill and then to a taxi or the guest's car
   • to the coach (if the guest is travelling in a party)
   • into storage (if the guest will be calling later to collect it)
   • direct to the guest's car (the bill has been settled and the guest has brought the car to the entrance to be loaded up).
4. Always take care when handling luggage. It may be heavier than it looks. Furnishings, decorations, suitcases and their contents can easily be damaged through careless handling. Unattended luggage is a security risk. (See unit 37.)
5. Issue receipts (if this is the procedure) for luggage taken into safe keeping. Otherwise ensure that left luggage is clearly identified with the name of the owner.
6. If guest luggage is to be left in a hotel bedroom (when the guest will usually be expected to pay the normal room tariff) ensure the room is marked unavailable for letting, and that access is restricted to authorised staff. This may involve double locking the room.

> **‼ REMEMBER**
>
> - Dishonest intentions can sometimes be revealed by the state of a person's luggage (see unit 37).
> - Luggage is one of the few forms of security an establishment has against a customer who does not pay the bill (see unit 49).
> - Luggage left outside guest rooms – say they are members of a group and the luggage has to be collected and taken down to the coach ready for an early departure – can pose a security risk. Professional hotel thieves who know this to be the practice will make a point of being around in order to collect likely valuables. Opportunist thieves will quickly take advantage of any such lapse in security.

Group departures

If a group of people will be checking out at the same time, pre-planning and special procedures will ensure the operation runs smoothly.

- An area can be set aside for the luggage to be left before it is loaded into the coach.

- The co-operation of the tour leader can ensure that everyone in the group has their luggage ready for collection at a convenient time.

- Group members should be informed via the tour leader of the procedure for paying for extras charged to individual room accounts. If the sums involved are likely to be substantial find out in advance how each person will be paying. The required authorisation can then be obtained in good time.

- If the main bill for the group will be sent to the tour operator for paying, for example, obtain any necessary authorisation from the tour leader in good time.

- If group members are responsible for paying their own accommodation bills, then in addition to the normal questions asked when guests register (see units 35 and 36), ask people sharing a room (say Miss Webster and Miss Forsyth) if they will be paying separately.

> **▶ ▶ ▶ TO DO**
>
> A large tour is staying in your hotel, the first of a series booked for the holiday season. You have been asked to discuss the departure arrangements with the rather anxious tour leader. Draw up a checklist covering what will be done by the hotel to make the departure process quick and trouble-free, and what you would like the members of the tour and the tour leader to do.

Methods of taking payment vary with the type of establishment. A leisure centre, theatre, cinema, holiday centre or night club would normally take payment before the customer uses the services, and extras such as ice cream in the interval or a bottle of wine would be paid for as required (and before consuming them). A restaurant, unless it is self service, normally takes payment after the customer has eaten. An establishment which offers overnight accommodation such as a motel or hotel would normally take payment at the end of the guest's stay, which may involve several days' expenses in food, drink, sleeping accommodation and other services.

Customers pay by:	
• cash	• credit card
• cheque	• account
• direct debit card	• travel agent's voucher.

The information in units 44 to 48 will help you gain the Caterbase modules *Handling Cash* and *Recording and Balancing Departmental Charges.*

General procedure

1. With billing machines and manual systems the bills are kept in a special tray or drawer, usually separated by metal or cardboard plates which have a tag at the top to indicate the room number.
2. With computer systems the details of each guest's bill are kept in the computer's memory and printed out on request. This may be the morning of the guest's departure, or at the time of departure. If the bill is printed in advance and the guest incurs a further charge, for example for breakfast, a new bill will have to be printed and the earlier version cancelled through by hand (it should only be torn up if there is no serial number on the bills).
3. When the guest has already signed a credit card voucher the amount can be completed once the guest has had time to study the bill. The guest should be given a copy of the completed voucher.
4. But if the guest decides instead to settle the account in cash or with a cheque the credit card voucher must be destroyed in the presence of the guest. When advance authorisation has been given, the credit card company must be informed of the cancellation.
5. The charge vouchers are filed – either with the bill or separately in a special tray or pigeon holes by room number. Some establishments only give the vouchers to guests if they ask for them (the most convenient procedure if the bill is printed on a computer). They may then be kept for a short time in case of a later query. Other establishments give the vouchers to guests alongside the bill.

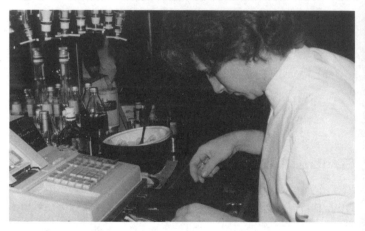

If money that the customers pay is mislaid or stolen, this can have a serious effect on the business. For this reason, many organisations use sophisticated point of sales equipment (cash tills) which keep a record of all cash paid. Those linked to a computer can show how sales are made up, for example, which services or items are selling well, and how those sales compare with the same period the previous year. This information is useful to management for financial planning

Most departures and check outs from establishments offering overnight accommodation occur between 7.30 and 9.30 in the morning. This can be a very busy time for the receptionist who will need to be organised if the procedure is to go smoothly and efficiently

Disputes

Sometimes the customer will disagree with the receptionist about the amount on the bill for instance, or the change given.

- Never become aggressive or argue with the person.
- Try and sort out the cause by checking the bill, the relevant vouchers, the change given, and so on.
- If there is a mistake apologise sincerely and do whatever is necessary to correct the mistake immediately.
- If you think the bill/change given is correct and the customer still disputes the amount, remain polite towards the guest, for instance offer a seat and say that you will check with the manager or supervisor.

Often the relevant charge voucher signed by the guest will show where the disputed amount came from, for instance when something was charged to the account after a late night drink in the night club.

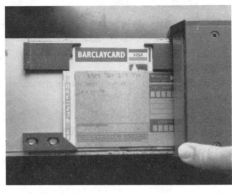

If a guest will be paying by credit card, an imprint of the card should be made when the guest checks in (see unit 36). Then authorisation can be obtained shortly before the guest is due to depart and as soon as the likely total of the bill has been established

 GUESTCRAFT TIPS

If guest bills have to be handwritten or printing them out is slow or difficult to arrange when several people want their bills at the same time, prepare the bills in advance as far as possible. It is easier to make an adjustment or print out a replacement bill for the odd person who has had a late charge than it is to leave every bill to be prepared at the last minute.

If a guest has been staying for a number of days and each day had similar items charged to the bill – for example a newspaper, breakfast served in the room, use of the minibar – but on the day of departure these items do not appear on the bill, check the reason. It could be that the voucher has not yet come through. Be careful not to offend the guest by tactless questioning. It is quite possible that someone facing a long journey has decided on the last day to have a full breakfast in the restaurant (the cost of which is covered in the accommodation charge). Or the person may have gone out to the pub as a final celebration and not used anything from the minibar.

* FOR INTEREST

Some establishments employ a runner to pick up late charges from all departments and make sure they arrive at the front desk before the peak check-out time. Others have pneumatic tubes which whisk the details from each department directly to the check-out desk.

 TO DO

Role play the following situations with two other colleagues or friends.

1. Dispute over a bill
Cast Receptionist, Customer, Manager
Situation A customer disputes the bill. The aim of the receptionist and manager is to convince the customer that the bill is correct.
Discussion points Did the customer agree with the bill in the end? How did the customer feel he or she was treated? Could the customer care skills of the receptionist and manager be improved upon?

2. A charge is missed from a guest bill
Cast Angelo (receptionist), Olga (restaurant manager), Alan James (hotel manager)
Situation Mr Agnew tells Angelo that he will be staying for two nights, but on the second evening immediately after eating dinner in the hotel restaurant he has to leave unexpectedly. He

checks out. But the late charge of £12 for dinner was not posted to his bill. Olga is always saying how proud she is that the restaurant operation has made a profit since she came to work at the Grand Hotel. She is understandably very upset when she realises the receptionist had forgotten to post the late charge to Mr Agnew's bill. Olga works out that the restaurant would need to generate an additional £150 in sales in order to make up for the £12 revenue which was never collected. When Angelo offers to chase up the missing amount by contacting Mr Agnew, Alan James, the hotel manager, tells him that the cost of doing this will probably be more than the £12 sum in question, what with the postage, telephone calls, stationery and the labour involved.
Discussion points What steps could be taken to prevent this situation from occurring again? Is Olga right that her department's revenue will be lower as a result of the unpaid bill (see units 47 and 48)?

Cash

Cash is the easiest form of money for someone to steal or mislay. It is also the most difficult to trace if a mistake is made. If a customer enters the wrong year on a cheque the person can normally be traced to correct the error. On the other hand, if a receptionist gives £5 too much in change and the customer does not say anything, the missing £5 will never be traced.

Always check large denomination notes for forgeries.

All cash should be kept locked up when not in use, and only certain people will have access to the key. Some organisations issue personal keys to staff and insist these are worn on the person for security. (See unit 54.)

Cheques

Most banks and building societies will guarantee to honour personal cheques up to a certain limit provided they are accompanied by a guarantee card. (This card may also serve the customer as a credit card, for example Barclaycard, or as a direct debit card, for example Connect.) Special arrangements between the customer and establishment and possibly the customer's bank, will usually have to be made in advance for greater amounts, and for accepting a cheque drawn on a company account. To avoid fraud make sure:

- the establishment accepts personal cheques
- the date on the cheque card has not expired
- the name on the card is the same as the name on the cheque
- the cheque comes from the same bank as the card (with some banks the code number of the issuing branch of the bank is on the card and the cheque – they should be the same)
- the value of the cheque is not more than the limit stated on the card, say £100 or £50
- the cheque is completed in permanent ink (any colour)
- the amounts in words and in figures on the cheque agree
- the cheque is dated correctly (usually with the date of the transaction). Postdated cheques should not be accepted as the account might be closed in the meantime
- the signature on the cheque is the same as that on the card, and the signature on the card has not been tampered with. If you are in any doubt ask the customer to sign again on the back of the cheque. If still unsure ask the customer politely to wait while you get your supervisor
- you write the cheque card number on the back of the cheque, the expiry date of the card and your initials
- you only accept one cheque for each transaction. If the bill comes to more than the limit stated on the card the customer should be asked to pay the difference in cash or by credit card, or check with your manager
- you only accept a company cheque which has been endorsed with the authorisation of your manager (see unit 60)
- any amendments to the cheque (for example a correction to the date) are endorsed with the initials of the customer.

The way customers pay for products and services depends on the type of establishment, and often the size of the bill. Cash is a common way of paying smaller bills, say for a round of drinks in a bar. Larger amounts can conveniently be paid by cheque and many establishments have facilities to exchange foreign currency and travellers' cheques

The information in units 45 and 46 will help you gain the Caterbase module *Handling Credit Facilities and Foreign Exchange.*

USEFUL TERM

Float A certain sum in notes and coins issued to the front office staff responsible for taking payment (see unit 48). The float should be large enough to give change when guests settle their bills, change foreign currency or cash travellers' cheques. In some establishments there is one float and one cash drawer which all the staff on duty have access to. Alternatively each person has a separate cash drawer and his or her own float.

Eurocheques are issued by banks for use in other countries. The traveller can issue cheques in specific currencies approved in advance by the bank. The actual amount paid by the customer will vary according to the rate of exchange when the cheque is presented. Eurocheques must often be accompanied by a cheque guarantee card, and the upper limit (say £100) must be checked before payment is accepted. Otherwise the procedure is the same as for ordinary bank and building society cheques.

Foreign exchange

Guests may wish to change foreign currency into Sterling (£) and many hotels will provide this service. If not the guests or non-residents should be directed to the nearest bank or foreign exchange bureau.

It is important to know which currencies your establishment will accept. Some use a foreign exchange docket which gives details to the guest of the exchange rate given and the corresponding amount in Sterling, and the currency offered. The guest then signs to agree the transaction.

Establishments usually make a profit on foreign currency transactions and so rates of exchange are not the same as the figures given by banks, large building societies and newspapers (these can fluctuate on a daily basis). The customer will want to see the current rates of exchange being used by the establishment so it is helpful to have a list displayed at the reception desk. Each country has a different name and symbol which relates to its currency (the equivalent of Sterling and £) and the receptionist should be familiar with the most common of these

 HOW TO

Exchange foreign currency

1. Say a customer wants $50 (fifty US dollars) exchanged into Sterling (£), and the establishment's rate of exchange is $1.43 to each £1.

   Divide the number of dollars offered by the number of dollars to the pound

   $50 \div 1.43 = 34.97$

   so the customer should receive £34.97.

2. Say the customer wants to pay her bill of £26.90 in dollars, and rate of exchange is $1.43 to the £1.

   Multiply the amount of the bill by the number of dollars to the pound

   $26.90 \times 1.43 = 38.47$

   so the customer will pay $38.47 for her bill. Foreign coins cannot be accepted so in this example the customer would probably pay $40, and the overpayment, $1.53, would have to be converted back to Sterling:

   $1.53 \div 1.43 = 1.07$

   so the customer will get £1.07 change.

Travellers' cheques

These are issued by banks and travel agents in the traveller's own country and are available in most of the major currencies. They can usually be replaced if lost or stolen and are certainly safer than large amounts of cash. Each cheque is for a specific amount which is clearly indicated, say $20. The person signs each travellers' cheque as soon as possible. There is a space for a second signature when the cheque is cashed or used to pay a bill. The two signatures must match. Some establishments will also require the receptionist to check the traveller's signature and photograph in a passport.

Travellers' cheques should be converted from the currency in which they were issued to Sterling.

▶ ▶ ▶ **TO DO**

Complete the final step in this general procedure for giving change. A £10 note has been given by the customer to pay for magazines and newspapers costing £3.27.

1. State the total amount due for the purchases.
2. State clearly the value of the note handed over.
3. Place the £10 note on the clip on the till, or clearly visible and separate from the other money in the till.
4. Press the control keys on the till for £3.27.
5. Check on the visual display that this has been recorded correctly.
6. When the till drawer opens take out the right change in the least number of coins and notes possible. You may find it useful to count upwards from £3.27.
7. Place the £10 note in the till.
8. Close the till drawer.
9. Count the change clearly into the customer's hand, placing the coin of the smallest denomination first and the largest note last. Count upwards from £3.27 until you reach £10:
   Three pounds twenty seven and 1p ... three twenty eight
   Three twenty eight and ...

Credit cards

Larger bills are often paid by credit cards which usually allow higher limits than say ordinary cheques from the bank or building society. This is possible because checks on the person's credit-worthiness have already been carried out either by the bank or other organisation issuing the credit.

The receptionist should therefore know which credit cards the establishment accepts. He or she completes a sales voucher and imprints the credit card on it, and the customer signs it.

When the receptionist is satisfied that everything is in order, the card holder is given the appropriate copy of the signed sales voucher and the bill as a receipt. Another copy of the voucher goes to the bank or credit card company for payment (not necessary if there is a direct computer link at the time of the transaction).

Sometimes when you phone a credit card company or bank for authorisation you may be asked to retain the customer's card, usually because there is some query about the person's credit-worthiness. This can be embarrassing for the customer, you and your organisation if the situation is not well handled.

- Smile at the customer.
- Explain the situation (out of earshot of other customers).
- Suggest the customer contact the credit card company or bank and speaks to them directly (offer a phone with some privacy).
- Do not give the card to the customer.
- If you feel you cannot handle the situation ask the customer to wait while you fetch the manager or supervisor.

Direct debit cards

Direct debit cards are accepted by many of the establishments that accept credit cards – Switch and Connect are two examples. The main difference is for the card holder. The money is deducted directly from the person's current account, usually about three days after the transaction. In this respect it is like a cheque but there is no limit on the amount, provided there are sufficient funds in the person's account. For the receptionist the procedure is similar to accepting payment by credit card, and authorisation must be sought from the issuing bank for amounts over a pre-set limit.

Accounts

Some bills are not paid immediately but sent on to the customer or company for payment. For those on business it means they do not have to pay the bill out of their own pocket and wait until they can claim expenses before being reimbursed. (Some companies issue their staff with a credit card such as American Express on the understanding that it is reserved for paying business expenses. This avoids the need to open accounts with a large

The analaysis of guest bills is made easier when the details are built up from the time the charge is first entered. On a manual system each charge will be written under the appropriate column on the tabular ledger, say 'Bars'. On a billing machine or computer the charge can only be added to the guest bill after depressing the appropriate department key, say 'Tel' or code, say 12 for laundry

To avoid fraud check that:
- the card is not stolen by consulting a list of stolen card numbers which should be kept at reception
- the date on the card has not expired
- you have noted the name on the card
- the signature on the voucher is the same as the one on the card. The customer must sign in front of you. Keep the specimen signature on the card out of sight while this is done. This makes it more difficult for a dishonest person to copy the signature
- if the amount of the account exceeds a certain limit (that set by the credit card company for normal acceptance, sometimes called the floor or house limit), obtain authorisation from the issuing company:
  - phone the credit card company
  - state your establishment reference number
  - give the card number
  - tell the credit card operator the amount to be charged to the account
  - write the authorisation code on the voucher

  (If your establishment has a direct link with the credit card company's computers authorisation will be automatic, provided the amount is within the account holder's credit limit, see unit 20.)
- you have imprinted the credit card on to the correct sales voucher
- all the necessary details have been recorded correctly on the voucher and any copies.

The information in this unit will help you gain the Caterbase module *Handling Credit Cards.*

Guest bills should always give sufficient detail for the guest to know what each charge relates to. What sort of detail is kept by the establishment will depend on management policy – sales and cost control are more accurate if different types of income and different categories of cost are kept separate

number of hotels.)

- Ask the guest to examine the bill and sign that he or she authorises it for payment by the account holder.
- Keep account (ledger) bills separate from bills paid at the time of departure.
- Attach a copy of the customer's letter of confirmation to the signed bill. (This makes it easier for the person responsible for collecting payment, often the control office, to deal with any query.)

Discount cards

Some establishments give a discount, for instance 10%, to certain customers on the basis their account is settled on departure and paid by cash or cheque. Those with a company/hotel discount card (issued to regular customers or shareholders, for example) or a cash discount card such as Countdown should present the card when they are settling the bill. The receptionist deducts the appropriate discount – which may be off the whole bill or off certain categories of expenditure, for instance accommodation only, or accommodation, restaurant, wines and drinks.

‼ REMEMBER

- If you accept payment for a bill larger than the upper limit allowed by the card the bank or credit card company is not obliged to honour the amount and your establishment could lose money.
- Blacklists or stoplists which contain details of stolen cheque books and cards, credit cards, travellers' cheques and so on are circulated to establishments by the major banks and credit card organisations. A list should always be kept in a discreet place at reception, and every card number should be checked against it.
- If you think you have caught someone trying to defraud your organisation, contact the manager without alerting the customer. A smile and 'I won't keep you a moment, Madam' will suffice. Never accuse the person. You may be putting your safety at risk

---

Travel agent's voucher

If the guest produces a travel agent's voucher the details should be checked with the establishment's own copy of the voucher (sent when the booking was made, see unit 33). The voucher will state the arrangements for paying – for example the whole bill is to be sent to the travel agent, or the guest has to pay for everything except the basic accommodation charge. The guest's copy is then usually kept by the establishment (arrangements vary according to the company issuing the voucher), and used to support the claim for reimbursement sent to the travel agent in due course.

▶▶▶ TO DO

Ask the local police to give you details on people who are known to be using stolen cheques and credit cards in your area. (You may need to explain why you want the information.) How do people manage to get hold of these items? What systems do they use so they won't get found out when obtaining cash and goods with them? What advice can the police give to organisations such as yours about protecting themselves from fraud?

There are three reasons for balancing up:
- to extract totals for the various types of charge and payments
- to check that no cash has gone astray
- as a first check for incorrect entries, omissions or other errors – those of the sort which prevent the debit charges and credit charges from balancing.

When balancing up is done at the end of the business day the total charges under various account headings (accommodation charges, bars, meals, laundry and so forth), and the total payments received and allowances made, are printed out and compared. Provided they balance, each account is re-set to zero.

When balancing up is done at another time, for example at the end of the morning shift, the readings are in effect sub-totals.

Computers and billing machines greatly reduce the chance of making errors

Examples of debit charges	Examples of credit charges
On individual guest bills	*Under department headings*
Accommodation only charge	Accommodation sales
Bed and breakfast charge	Accommodation sales (for value of accommodation)
	Coffee shop sales (for value of breakfast)
Drinks (bar)	Bar sales
Meal	Restaurant sales
Wines	Bar sales
Telephone	Telephone sales
Under account headings	*On individual guest bills*
Cash received	Payment
Advance deposit	Deposit
Guest ledger	Balance carried forward to next day (for guests staying more than one day)

  TO DO

Find out from three contrasting hotels what department headings guest charges are allocated to. What are the differences and similarities?

General procedure

At the end of the business day, and perhaps at the end of a shift, the total amounts charged to each department are compared with the total owed by guests less payments and allowances made during the period. A computer will carry out the process automatically as soon as it is given the appropriate instruction. Billing machines will give the totals when set in a particular mode of operation (for example by turning a key to 'x reading'). With tabular ledgers it is a matter of adding up the various columns.

USEFUL TERMS

Business day The period of time which is considered to make up a particular day. This starts when the totals under each account or department heading are set at zero and ends when the totals are recorded and the accounts balanced. In small or medium sized hotels the business day may end at 11 p.m. when the late shift finishes. Any charges incurred by guests during the night (for example a late night snack served by the night porter) will be treated as income earned in the following day. In some establishments the night auditors or a duty manager will take the readings and re-set account categories to zero during the early hours of the morning.

x reading When a billing or accounting machine is required to give a total of any or all account categories.

z reading After the totals in the various account categories have been printed out with an x reading, each account is re-set to zero with a z reading. This is only done at the end of the business day, usually after errors which prevent the debit and credit amounts from balancing have been corrected. On most machines a z reading can only be taken by certain people (for example the head receptionist or night auditor) who have access to a special key or know the password.

Hidden charge The proportion of an inclusive tariff that is assigned to cover the cost of breakfast, and if included, lunch and dinner. Part of the accounting system may include the transfer of these charges from accommodation revenue to restaurant revenue (and any other appropriate departments). It is not necessary or usual to show the breakdown on guest bills, hence the expression 'hidden'.

Ledger or **suspense account** Used in front office operations to describe the transfer of an unpaid guest bill to a separate ledger or account heading called outstanding accounts ledger, for example, or debtors ledger. There it is held until settled (see unit 46).

Visitors paid out or **VPO** When money is paid out of petty cash on behalf of the guest, for example to have the guest's car washed and filled with petrol. The amount is added to the guest's bill.

Balancing up	For example		
		£	£
1. Total each debit (that is department) account.	Accommodation	1500	
	Restaurant	900	
	Bars	850	
2. Sub-total the debit accounts.		3250	
3. Add to this the total brought forward from the previous day as the amount owed by people staying on.		750	
4. Find the new sub-total to establish the total owed.		4000	
5. Total each credit account: payment received, allowances made, transfers to ledger	Payment		960
	Allowances		50
	Ledger		150
6. Deduct the credit total (5) from the amount charged to guests (4) to find the total amount guests are due to pay.		1160 2840	1160
7. Work through all the outstanding guest bills adding the amount owing on each to get a total of the amount guests are due to pay.	Paul Jones	1100	
	Mrs Smith	140	
	Mr Harding	250	
	T G Lines & Co	1350 2840	
8. Check that the two calculations of amounts to be paid by guests are identical, that is balance.	From records	2840	
	From bills	2840	

If the amounts do not balance

With a tabular ledger and some billing machines it can take quite a time to discover where the error has been made. Start with the simpler checks:

- Have any bills been misfiled?
- Have any paid bills been left in the outstanding bill tray in error? (If paid bills end with a zero balance, or they are clearly marked as paid this sort of error should be spotted earlier.)
- Does the discrepancy match a particular charge? Say there is a £15 difference, this could mean that a restaurant charge for £15 was added to a guest bill but not entered in the appropriate column in the tabular ledger. If the charge has been entered in the tabular ledger, it might have been put on a second guest bill by mistake, or it might not have been put on a guest bill at all. A discrepancy of £85 could mean that the balance on a particular bill was not brought forward from the previous day. It might also mean that the balance was not entered on the billing machine before the new charge was added (when this is not done automatically).
- An error in addition or subtraction has been made (manual systems only).

When the amounts balance

At the end of the business day the totals are finally read and then re-set to zero (on a billing machine this is known as a 'z reading'). The amounts outstanding on guest bills are carried forward to the next day.

If the various accounts do not balance at the end of a shift it is usual for the staff concerned to remain on duty until the problem has been found and corrected. If the amount of cash is over or under what it should be, and the reason cannot be found, the difference is noted as under/overbanking.

The information in this unit, units 19 and 48 will help you gain the Caterbase module *Handling Sales Ledger*.

```
        X BALANCES
        TOTALS NOT RESET
        GEORGE HOTEL
        HIGH STREET COLCHESTER
        02407805
        . . . . . . . . . . . . . . . . .
        GRAND TOTAL
              13       476.19 DR
               1        45.68 CR
        TOTAL           430.51 DR
        . . . . . . . . . . . . . . . . .
        DINERS CLUB INTL
               1        21.60 DR
               0         0.00 CR
        TOTAL 0221-0222  21.60 DR
        . . . . . . . . . . . . . . . . .
        AMERICAN EXPRESS
               5       164.46 DR
               0         0.00 CR
        TOTAL 0564-0569 164.46 DR
        . . . . . . . . . . . . . . . . .
        ACCESS
               2        58.18 DR
               0         0.00 CR
        TOTAL 0941-0943  58.18 DR
        . . . . . . . . . . . . . . . . .
        VISA
               5       231.95 DR
               1        45.68 CR
        TOTAL 1251-1257 186.27 DR
```

Using the correct vouchers when imprinting credit cards will increase the chance of getting a successful result when the x reading is done. It also reduces the risk of claiming from the wrong company. When this happens most credit card companies will send the voucher to the correct company but inevitably this slows up payment to the establishment

Correcting overcharges

An overcharge relating to a previous day's business is treated as an *allowance*. Say on Thursday Mr Creswick of room 232 queries a charge of £10.50 for use of the minibar on Wednesday. It turns out the charge should have been put on the bill of room 223 (Mrs Hill). An allowance of £10.50 on Mr Creswick's bill will reduce the amount he has to pay and details are recorded (usually on an allowance voucher or docket) of the amount and reason. If Mrs Hill has already left the hotel the amount is charged to a special walk-out ledger account and in due course written off.

On the other hand if Mrs Hill is still staying in the hotel the charge will be put on her bill as an *adjustment*.

Handing over the float

The value of the float should never change. However the value of money in the cash drawer or till will:

- increase every time a customer pays a bill (whether it be in cash, by credit card, cheque or in foreign exchange)
- decrease if cash is given to staff in exchange for a petty cash voucher, for example
- be unaffected by foreign currency exchanges

and so, at any time, the value of money in the cash drawer or till should equal:

- the value of the float

plus

- the total of all bills paid by customers.

When responsibility for the cash drawer and/or float changes, say at the end of a shift, the value should be carefully checked. Only when the total agrees with what it should be can the new staff accept responsibility.

Generally at shift changes, and always at the end of the business day, the difference between the float and what is in the drawer is put in a safe. There it is kept securely until it can be taken to the bank. The amount must agree with the total paid by customers during the shift. (On a billing machine or computer this can be found by sub-totalling the cash taken, on a tabular ledger the figures in the cash column are totalled.)

If the float gets short of coins and low denomination notes, then some of the notes will need to be exchanged for coins to the same value. The larger establishments will keep change in the main cashier's office (or in the manager's safe) for this purpose. If a lot of foreign currency has been exchanged this may make it difficult for giving change until the notes can be turned back into Sterling currency.

Some computerised front office accounting systems will convert a transaction into a foreign currency. Say the guest wishes to pay in US$, the bill total will be converted from Sterling into Dollars at the current exchange rate (programed into the computer each day). The change will be automatically calculated from the Dollar amount tendered by the guest, and converted back into Sterling so the correct change can be given to the guest in Sterling.

This system also makes cashing up easier. The value of various foreign notes and travellers' cheques is converted into Sterling showing the balance that has to be handed over in Sterling to leave the float correct

---

The term 'adjustment' is sometimes used instead of 'allowance'. What should be remembered is that corrections to guest bills have to be made in such a way that the totals for the account headings concerned are not over-stated. The fact that £10.50 of minibar sales on Wednesday were charged to the wrong room number does not decrease the sales. But if the error was spotted on Thursday and the £10.50 was added to Mrs Hill's bill as minibar sales then the sale would be counted twice: once on Wednesday and again on Thursday.

In some establishments the front office is responsible for issuing floats to other departments such as the bar and restaurant. The float should be handed over in a secure area and double checked by the person taking over responsibility. A float book is a useful way of recording the date and time of handovers, with space for the signatures of the recipient as well as the person handing it over.

If the takings are also handed to the front office for safekeeping and perhaps banking, they will be checked carefully before responsibility is accepted. The takings will usually be entered in a cash received book and in due course banked with the takings from other departments and reception itself.

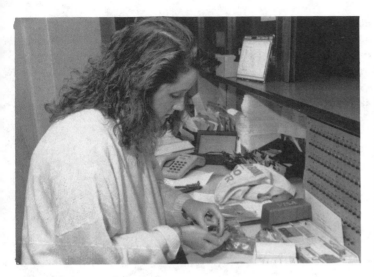

Banking procedure

- Most establishments will bank payments received from customers daily, or twice daily. It is a security risk to keep large amounts of cash on the premises (see unit 54). It also makes better business sense for money to be in the bank as soon as possible. The cheque clearing process can begin promptly, and the money can be used to finance supplies, pay wages, reduce borrowings or increase savings which earn interest.

- The money to be banked is counted and itemised on the paying-in slip, with separate totals for cheques and cash. Generally the cheques are listed on the back of the paying-in slip, and a breakdown may be given of each denomination of note and coin to make counting easier.

- Staples should be removed from cheques. Notes should be kept the same way up, with the Queen's portrait on the top and bundled together in £100 amounts. (An elastic band or paper clip will keep the notes together.) Scottish bank notes should be kept separate.

- Coins should be kept in separate plastic, cloth or paper bags. Special bags are available from banks which hold a specific value, say £10 in 50p coins. The cashier then weighs the bag and provided the weight is correct for the type of coin and value there is no need to recount them.

- Foreign exchange is paid in separately, as the bank will have to calculate the Sterling equivalent (usually different from the exchange rate used for hotel guests).

- Credit card vouchers are sent to the credit card company concerned unless it is a bank credit card (such as Access or Barclaycard when they are paid into a bank in a similar way to cheques).

The information in this unit will help you gain the Caterbase module *Banking*.

Departmental control

When a hotel guest in the bar, for example, signs a drinks voucher for the amount to be added to her bill, a record is kept in the bar before the voucher is sent to the front office. This record often consists of a duplicate copy of the voucher. Alternatively the cash till in the bar records the payment details for each sale (in this case the room number it has been charged to). At the end of the business day the barman's total for what has been charged to guest bills should be exactly the same as the total charged to guest bills for drinks by the front office staff.

The bar's record of individual amounts charged to guest bills (from copies of the vouchers or the printed record of transactions on the cash till) will be compared at a later stage with the front office records. This may be done by control office staff (for example in a large organisation), by management or by the auditors. Usually only a sample will be compared, but if discrepancies are found a full check is likely to follow.

▶▶▶ TO DO

Arrange through your tutor or supervisor to be present when a typical day's banking is prepared. If possible choose an establishment where the takings include foreign currency and travellers' cheques as well as ordinary cheques, notes and coins. Make a note of the security precautions which are taken and of any tips you are given on how to handle large sums of money confidently, accurately and quickly.

XI Data Systems				THE XITEL DEMONSTRATION HOTEL			
				SALES ANALYSIS SUMMARY FOR 01NOV			
ACCOMMODATION SALES	Week to Date			Period to Date			
	Sales	Qty	Unit Value	Sales	Qty	Unit Value	
ACCOMMODATION	162.70	2	81.35	162.70	2	81.35	
ACCOMMODATION CONFERENCES	426.11	14	30.43	426.11	14	30.43	
ACCOMMODATION PACKAGES	47.82	3	15.94	47.82	3	15.94	
ACCOMMODATION SALES	636.63	19	33.50	636.63	19	33.50	
Subtotal for Section "A"	636.63	19	33.50	636.63	19	33.50	
FOOD SALES	Week to Date			Period to Date			
	Sales	Qty	Unit Value	Sales	Qty	Unit Value	
DINNER CONFERENCES	119.57	14	8.54	119.57	14	8.54	
FOOD SALES	119.57	14	8.54	119.57	14	8.54	
Subtotal for Section "F"	119.57	14	8.54	119.57	14	8.54	
TOTAL	756.20	33	22.91	756.20	33	22.91	

Information from the front office is analysed in a variety of ways by management to maintain effective sales and cost control

The Hotel Proprietors Act (1956) Most hotels, motels, inns and guest-houses are covered under the Act's definition of an inn. Their proprietors and staff are under an obligation to offer at any time of the day or night:
- accommodation – if required and provided the hotel is not full
- reasonable refreshment – provided it is not the last food and drink in the hotel and provided it is something within the hotel's ability to provide (a hot meal when the kitchens are closed and the staff have gone off duty would be an unreasonable request)

to any traveller who appears to be:
- in a fit state to be received (a very drunk person or a person suffering from a contagious disease could therefore be refused)
- able and willing to pay a reasonable sum for the services provided (judging this can be difficult, unless the person has none or very little luggage, when advance payment can be insisted on).

Liability for guest property
A hotel is liable for loss (which includes theft) or damage of guest property which occurs during a period of one night or more when the person is booked to stay, commencing from midnight immediately before and ending midnight immediately after the stay.
- The schedule of the Hotel Proprietors Act must be displayed as a notice in a prominent place in the reception/main entrance area.
- Liability for guest property is generally limited to £50 for any one article and £100 for any one claim.
- If guests' property deposited with the hotel for safekeeping is lost or damaged, the hotel is fully liable.
- If the hotel refuses to accept valuables offered by guests for safekeeping, the proprietor is liable for their full value if they are subsequently lost or damaged because of this refusal. The hotel has the right to insist that the valuables are placed in a container and sealed by the guest before being accepted by the hotel.
- The hotel is fully liable if the guest can prove that the loss or damage was the result of wilful damage caused by the proprietor or the proprietor's staff, or their negligence or default.
- The hotel is not liable for guest property when it can prove that the loss or damage was caused by total negligence on the part of the guest, or an act of God or the Queen's enemies.
- Cars parked on hotel property without payment of a parking fee, property left in guest's cars, horses and other animals belonging to guests are not protected.

Customers who use the hotel restaurant or bar for example but do not stay in the hotel are not covered by the Hotel Proprietors Act. Boarding houses, private hotels, guesthouses and leisure centres do not come within the legal definition of a hotel if they only accept guests/residents by prior contract. The normal laws of contract and negligence apply in these cases.

People staying in licensed hotels and other establishments offering overnight accommodation can purchase alcohol for themselves at any time of the day or night, provided the licensee agrees to serve them. In these circumstances, residents can also purchase alcohol for their friends (but not vice versa)

 TO DO

Outline the action you would take if a customer arrived at the reception desk and asked for a room for the night. The customer is scruffy and smells of alcohol.

Then with a partner act out the scene, with other group members commenting on your handling of the situation.

Alternatively
With some colleagues make up three or four examples of hotel brochure descriptions that would be misleading and could lead to a prosecution under the Trades Descriptions Act. If there is a cartoonist in the group to illustrate the ideas, all the better.

Then re-write the descriptions so that they are truthful but still present the hotel in an attractive way to potential customers.

The Innkeepers Act (1878) Common law gives a hotel the right to retain luggage (but not cars) belonging to a guest who is unable to pay his or her bill. Luggage to the value of the unpaid bill can be kept until the bill is paid. If the bill has not been paid after six weeks the Innkeepers Act gives the hotel the right to sell the goods by public auction. The date and location of the sale must be advertised:

- in one London and one local newspaper
- at least one month in advance
- with a short description of the items intended to be sold
- with the name of the owner or person who left the items.

The hotel must return to the guest any money left over after the bill has been paid and the hotel's expenses have been recovered.

Where young people can drink alcohol

Young people over 14 and under 18 are allowed in a bar, but they cannot be served with alcohol nor consume it in a bar.

Young people over 16 may buy and drink beer or cider with a meal in a part of the premises set aside for the service of food (not the bar). They are allowed to buy tobacco and cigarettes from the bar.

Young people under 16 are allowed to be in a restaurant, dining room or eating area set apart and used exclusively for eating meals when alcohol is only served or consumed as an ancillary to the meal. They may not purchase alcoholic drinks, but they may, at the licensee's discretion, be allowed to drink alcohol with a table meal provided it is purchased by an accompanying adult (a parent or other responsible guardian).

Children under 14 are allowed into areas which are part of licensed premises which are used for purposes other than drinking, such as a hotel lounge or restaurant (but not a bar).

The Tourism (Sleeping Accommodation Price Display) Order (1977) This Act requires accommodation charges to be advertised so they can be seen before guests register. The notice must state the price for each type of room inclusive of service charge and show the VAT element. The notice must indicate clearly what the price includes, for example breakfast. If there is a range of prices, the minimum and maximum prices should be shown.

The Trades Description Act (1968) Misleading or untrue descriptions of goods and services for sale (made verbally or in writing) are illegal under this Act and may lead to criminal prosecution.

Contract law The law protects both the customer and the establishment from unfair treatment by the other party to a contract.

A contract may be verbal (but this may be difficult to prove) or written. There are two stages and usually two parties, typically the customer (or someone acting on behalf of the customer, for instance a travel agent) and the establishment.

The offer For example a guest asks the receptionist if a single room is available for the night. The receptionist replies that there is and states the charge for bed and breakfast.

The acceptance The moment the guest accepts the receptionist's offer a contract is formed. If the guest replies the room is too expensive the receptionist may make a new offer, say for a single room without bath. If this is accepted a contract will exist. If the offer is made by post – in answer to a guest's letter of enquiry, for example – a contract exists from the moment the guest posts the letter of acceptance (confirming the booking). It is therefore advisable to qualify offers 'subject to the accommodation being available at the time of receipt of the reply'.

A booking can be cancelled provided the other party is notified in reasonable time to make alternative arrangements. What is considered reasonable will be judged on the normal booking pattern so a seaside hotel will usually need longer notice of a cancellation than an airport hotel.

If the customer cancels a booking the cancellation takes effect at the time the letter is posted.

On the other hand when a hotel makes the cancellation it only takes effect when the customer receives notification.

When a guest's booking is made by a travel agent or other third party, both the guest and the agent are liable. But if the agent discloses the name of the guest at the time of making the booking, the agent has no liability.

If either party defaults on a contract – in other words does not keep to its side of the arrangement – the injured party may sue for compensation.

A number of hoteliers and restaurateurs have successfully sued customers for breach of contract. They welcome the publicity this brings, feeling customers must learn to treat bookings more seriously

Non-British passport holders have to provide certain additional details when they register, but foreign diplomats, their families and staff are exempt

The Diplomatic Privileges Act (1964) Foreign diplomats, their families and staff are exempted by this Act from the need to register at a hotel.

The Race Relations Act (1976) This Act makes it illegal to discriminate against anyone (customers or employees) because of their race or nationality.

The Immigration (Hotel Records) Order (1972)
This states that for any person over the age of 16 (unless exempted by the Diplomatic Privileges Act) certain details must by provided verbally or in writing to any hotel in which the person will be staying. A travel agent or other third party can provide the information on the person's behalf. The following details must be recorded in writing, if necessary by the receptionist:

- full name
- nationality
- date of arrival

and for non-British passport holders:

- number and place of issue of passport, registration certificate or other document establishing identity and nationality
- on or before their date of departure, inform the hotel of the address of their next destination if known.

If a number of people are sharing a room these details must be given for each person, even if they are husband and wife. However it is not illegal for someone to register under a false name.

Registration documents can be inspected at any time by the police or any person appointed by the Secretary of State for the Home Office. They must be kept by the establishment for at least 12 months.

Clubs, hospitals, schools and halls of residence do not come within the scope of the Order.

> ◗ ◗ ◗ **TO DO**
>
> Consider each of the following situations and if the law has been broken name the act and state what should have been done.
> - Mr and Mrs Joseph check into the hotel with their 16 year old son. Mr Jones completes the registration form in his name only.
> - Micky Wild a famous pop star and his current girlfriend check into the hotel under the name of Mr and Mrs Smith.
> - Fictitious UK Ltd, a large company, has a booking for 25 single rooms with private bathroom for 23rd of January. That morning at 10 a.m. the general manager's secretary telephones to cancel the booking.
> - Mrs Yokhomo, wife of the Japanese ambassador, checks into the hotel and refuses to sign the register.
> - A visitor from Israel is refused accommodation by the proprietor (who comes from a country in the Middle East which is hostile to the Jews).

This document fulfils three purposes: reservation record, registration form and bill

The law exists to protect the customers, staff and anyone else, such as motorbike messengers and taxi drivers, who use the premises. The law consists of several acts of parliament, some of which directly affect the health and safety aspects of the receptionist's work. (See also units 52, 53 and 54.)

Safety

The aim of the Health and Safety at Work Act (1974) is to make everyone working in an establishment responsible for safety.

The Act and regulations made under the Act require employers to:
- ensure the building and the people in it are as safe as possible
- train staff in safe working practices and the use of equipment
- keep an accident book and provide first aid facilities
- provide equipment and tools with proper safeguards, and repair or replace worn or badly maintained equipment
- provide safe systems for the use, handling, storage and transport of materials such as cleaning agents, food and drink items
- take immediate action if any safety hazard is reported
- provide a written statement or policy describing the arrangements made for the health and safety of staff

and employees have to co-operate, taking care that they do not endanger their own health and safety, nor that of other people who may be affected by the way they work.

Environmental health officers are the people who enforce the Health and Safety at Work Act in most of the industry. They have various options in cases where this law has been broken, including fining, imposing a prison sentence, or closing down the establishment. An employer and an employee can also be held personally responsible for an accident and may be prosecuted if found guilty of negligence.

Fire

Fire is the major threat to the safety and security of a building. Most fires result from smoking and matches, misuse of electrical equipment, faults in heating systems, and poor refuse systems. Some are small, but others result in injury and loss of life.

The Fire Precautions Act (1971) is the main piece of legislation controlling fire safety in occupied premises in Great Britain. This act covers:
- hotels, guesthouses and boarding houses where there is some sleeping accommodation above first

Say a receptionist were to ignore the flex on the electric typewriter, photocopier or computer that had damaged insulation and a colleague had an electric shock from it. If it could be proved that the receptionist was fully aware of this and had ignored it, he or she would be liable for damages as well as the proprietor

IN CASE OF A FIRE

To provide additional safety for Guests, this Hotel is provided with a Fire Alarm System.

IF YOU DISCOVER A FIRE:
1. Leave your room making sure the door is firmly closed behind you.
2. Immediately operate nearest Fire Alarm call-point.

FIRE ALARM AND EVACUATION PROCEDURE:
3. The signal to evacuate the building is a continuous sounding of the Fire Alarm. When you hear it, you should leave the building IMMEDIATELY using the nearest available exit or stairway and proceed to the assembly point in St. Martin's Street.

DO NOT STOP TO COLLECT PERSONAL BELONGINGS.

DO NOT USE THE LIFTS.

DO NOT RE-ENTER THE BUILDING.

IMPORTANT
Before you go to bed, make sure you know the means of escape in case of fire and know how and where to raise the alarm.
If your companion is incapacitated in such a manner that you would require assistance in an emergency, please notify Reception.

floor level or below ground floor level or sleeping accommodation for more than six people (whether staff or guests), on the ground floor

- restaurants, pubs, bars, offices and shops where more than 20 people work at any one time, or more than ten people work other than on the ground floor.

These premises must have a fire certificate, which is granted once the authorities are satisfied that the fire fighting equipment is adequate, and that proper precautions against fire have been taken, including training and the provision of adequate fire exits and fire warning systems.

Premises (but not hotels) which are ground floor premises, or ground and basement premises where the basement is separated from the ground floor by 30 minutes' fire-resisting materials, qualify for exemption from the need to have a fire certificate. But they do have to provide a means of escape and appropriate fire fighting equipment. The Home Office has issued a code of practice for such premises and failure to comply with the code can lead to the fire authority issuing an Improvement Notice. Failure to comply with such a notice is an offence.

The Data Protection Act (1984)

The increase in the use of computers has made access to all sorts of data (information) easier for others to obtain, including unscrupulous people. This Act regulates the use of personal data. It applies mainly to banks, building societies, insurance offices and those hotel, catering, leisure and tourism companies which hold large databases (including customer mailing lists). It also concerns staff records (employee details) when they are held on computer. The Act gives the individual the right of:

- access to his or her files held on computer
- deletion or correction of inaccurate information
- compensation for damages (which may mean the establishment is taken to court).

So it is important to get the information right if you are responsible for typing it into the computer. It is also essential to restrict who have access to this information. If you suspect anyone asking for data is not *bona fide* then you should check with management before allowing access.

▶ ▶ ▶ TO DO

Carry out a check of all the areas of your workplace or college to which you normally have access, and make a list of any hazards from fire or accident. How would you go about getting rid of these hazards?

‼ REMEMBER

Anyone writing to the establishment to ask for details of personal data held about him or her is entitled to receive this within 40 days. A charge of £10 can be made by the establishment to cover administration costs. If the deadline is not met the individual can complain to the data protection registrar or take the case to court. This can be very expensive for the establishment and disastrous for its reputation.

USEFUL TERM

Data Defined in the Data Protection Act as information in a form in which it can be processed automatically, such as on computer disc. In other words it would be easy to gain access to it unless steps are taken to protect it.

What causes accidents

Nearly all accidents are caused by human error:

- carelessness
- improper behaviour and dress
- drinking
- lack of training, supervision, or experience.
- thoughtlessness
- tiredness
- drug taking

Of course receptionists cannot be responsible for the behaviour and actions of everyone who uses the premises. But they can control their own way of behaving, and they can try to make it second nature to recognise a hazard wherever it occurs, and remove it or report it to management before anyone gets hurt.

- Keep the reception area clean, tidy and free from obstructions.
- Follow manufacturer's instructions when using equipment.
- Know what to do in the event of an emergency, fire or accident.
- Know what the law and the establishment requires of you to protect everyone using the premises.

Keeping healthy

Bacteria causing illness and disease thrive in dirty conditions. The reception area is particularly prone to dust and soil brought in from the street. Housekeeping staff may have the major responsibility for keeping the foyer clean, but the receptionist will probably have to deal with the smaller cleaning tasks, or those which happen unexpectedly, such as a spilt jug of milk.

One of the major sources of infection is the human body. So everyone has a responsibility to keep themselves clean and healthy (see unit 24). If you have an infectious illness, even just a cold, it is usually better to remain at home rather than infect your colleagues and customers. Customers are immediately put off by staff who are unkempt and unclean because it indicates that standards of hygiene in the establishment are low.

- Wash hands frequently especially after visiting the lavatory, blowing your nose, sneezing, smoking or eating.

See the Mastercraft book *Health, Hygiene and Safety in the Hotel and Catering Industry* and video *The Human Factor*.

The reception area is the centre of communication in the establishment. You may be required to phone the police, fire or ambulance service at any time during your working day. Prompt action may save a life

Staff as well as management have a legal (see unit 51) and moral obligation to do everything they can to look after their own safety and welfare, and that of their colleagues and customers

First aid

Employers are required by law to provide first aid equipment at the workplace. Specific members of staff are appointed either as qualified first aiders or as people who can take charge if there is an accident and no first aider is available. Make sure you know who your first aider is.

- Cover cuts, grazes and burns with a dressing.
- Never smoke in front of customers.
- Do not lick your fingers, scratch or touch your hair.
- Avoid blowing your nose, sneezing or yawning in public.

Using equipment

Equipment is less likely to go wrong if it is regularly maintained and used properly by staff who have been trained to do so. For instance the paper and ink used with photocopiers, bill printers and faxes should be of a type recommended by the manufacturers.

- If any equipment is faulty this should be reported immediately to the person in charge.
- If the equipment cannot be removed or repaired immediately a note saying 'out of order' or 'do not use' should be fixed to it because anyone using it could easily be hurt through say an electric shock when using a faulty word processor or light switch.

Planning your work

Staff who know what they have to do, work more efficiently and calmly, and are less likely to cause accidents or suffer injury. It may not be possible to avoid those times when several guests want to check out at the same time or a coach load of tourists arrives for a meal. But you can at least prepare yourself for most of these occasions. You can even plan to a certain extent for the unexpected.

- Be on time for the start of a shift (the handover) so that your colleagues can brief you properly and go off at the time they are meant to.
- Work to an overall plan so that you know which jobs need to be done first and which can wait. In this way the important tasks are not left till last, and urgent tasks get done in good time.
- Remember, accidents are more likely to happen when you are under pressure.

 TO DO

Visit three or four front of house or reception areas in establishments used by the public – say a restaurant, swimming pool, hospital and hotel foyer – and note any safety aspects incorporated into the architecture, design, decor and furnishings. Some examples may include fire exits, unbreakable glass, rounded edges to the reception desk. Are there any other safety features you would like to see included? Can you spot any outright hazards in their design?

The accident book
All accidents and illness at the workplace must by law be recorded in the accident book or on a suitable form (see illustration in unit 28). Details of each incident should include:
1. Date and time of incident.
2. Full name and occupation of person involved.
3. Nature of the injury or illness or dangerous occurrence.
4. Place where the incident happened and a brief description of what happened.
5. Names of any witnesses.
6. Details of the person making the report and time and date the report was made.

 HOW TO

Call for emergency assistance
1. Use any telephone: get an outside line if necessary and dial 999. No money is required if you are using a public call box.
2. Ask for the necessary service:
   - ambulance
   - fire brigade
   - police
3. When you get through give the telephone number so they can ring you back if the call gets cut off.
4. State the location and give as much detail as can be given quickly.
5. State the nature of the accident, for example a fall down a flight of stairs.
6. If it is a medical condition, such as a heart attack or a child birth, say so.
7. Remain on the phone until the emergency service rings off, to be sure you have given sufficient information.

Dealing with a death on the premises
Housekeeping, room service or reception staff may be the first to discover that the occupant of a room has died, or appears to be dead (he or she may be in a deep coma).

A doctor should be called at once and the police informed (this will usually be done by management as soon as the matter has been reported). The doctor and/or police will take care of arrangements such as informing the next of kin and removing the body. The reception staff may be asked to help gather the dead person's belongings, making a record of them in case of any uncertainty later, and packing them ready for collection by the next of kin.

If a death does occur in the building, everyone involved will usually be asked to act as discreetly as possible to avoid upsetting customers and other staff.

The reception area or foyer is by definition a public area. It is normally easy for anyone to gain access, simply by walking in. This is fine. The establishment wants and needs customers and everyone else necessary to the smooth running of the organisation – until the wrong person manages to get through. The security equipment and systems of establishments will vary in their effectiveness (see unit 23), but they are only as good as the people who use them.

Who goes there?

Most people will have a legitimate reason for being in the establishment – they are customers, service engineers, staff and so forth. And your establishment may keep a list of visitors who should not be allowed access. Customers who have been blacklisted because they have been abusive, violent, drunk or they have not paid their bill should be told politely and firmly that they are not welcome (see unit 37). But you cannot be expected to recognise everyone. Think of it this way: if a person entering the building is not a member of staff or a customer, that person could be a:

- thief
- prostitute
- drug pusher
- drunkard
- mugger
- rapist
- terrorist
- beggar
- con man.

Unless you are already sure what a person's business in the establishment is, you should find out by saying, for instance, 'May I help you?' If the person cannot give a legitimate reason and you become suspicious you should contact management or security immediately. In extreme cases it may be necessary to contact the police. But this should always be done as discreetly as possible so that other customers are not disturbed.

Callers such as meter readers, messengers, taxi drivers and service engineers, even if you recognise them, should be asked their business and, where appropriate, accompanied by a member of staff to their destination.

Can a suspect person be recognised?

The answer is 'probably'. Some can, some can't. It is possible to develop a sixth sense for recognising when something is wrong. It's a question of observing what people do and relating this to what people normally do in the same circumstance. For instance when customers enter the building for the first time they will probably make their way to the enquiries or reception desk. This is normal behaviour. A suspect person may try to walk straight up the stairs to the first floor. If you do not make the effort to observe what is going on, then you may have given the thief, rapist or terrorist the opportunity he or she was looking for.

Security in design

When a new building is planned, careful thought should go into security aspects such as the design of doors, windows and locks. Unfortunately many buildings were erected before the security risks of the twentieth century were even heard of. Receptionists should be aware of the layout of the public area where they work, and be extra vigilant if, for example, there are places hidden from view where suspect packages could be left.

Receptionists must follow the security procedures of their workplace when, for instance, issuing keys. They also need to develop the instincts of a detective – to become aware of the comings and goings through reception, to recognise faces, to have a good memory, to have a nose for suspicious circumstances, to be good at communicating with people. Being at the front desk they are in the best position to do so. Without these measures and skills the safety and security of everyone who uses the building, and their property, could be put at risk

Fire alarms, emergency telephones and emergency keys are generally located in reception. It is often the only area in a residential establishment that is staffed constantly throughout the day and night

Protecting guests

Guest room numbers should never be given out to strangers. If a caller arrives at the desk asking for a particular guest:

- obtain the caller's name (and company)
- offer a seat, if appropriate, while you contact the guest, probably by internal phone
- when the guest answers the call inform him or her of the identity and whereabouts of the caller
- tell the caller that the guest has been informed.

If there is no reply from the guest:

- ask the caller if he or she would like to leave a message or wait for the guest (see units 28 and 40).

Issuing keys to guests

Guest room keys must never be given out without first checking the identity of the person. In some establishments keys are only given out if the person produces a key card as proof of identity (see unit 13). Guests often forget to give in room keys, and it is the job of the receptionist to remind them when they check out. Housekeeping staff should hand into reception any keys left in guest rooms after the occupants have checked out.

Many establishments have computerised key systems which help to reduce theft because they are programmed to work for a particular guest rather than a particular room. After this they are discarded. (See unit 23.)

GUESTCRAFT TIPS

- Never allow master keys off the premises.
- Control stocks of blank key cards carefully so they do not fall into the wrong hands.
- Do not number or label keys so it is immediately obvious to anyone who might find them what lock(s) the key will open.
- Do not mark key tags with the full name and address of the establishment, in case the key falls into the wrong hands. A PO Box number can be arranged with the Post Office so that keys can be posted back by hotel guests who take them in error.
- Store guest room keys so that no-one can easily tell which guests are out. Avoid displays of carefully arranged keys with large tags indicating their room number and boxes underneath that show the guest is out because a message is waiting.
- Provide a posting box on the reception or porter's counter so guests can leave their keys on departure without any danger of someone else picking them up off the counter.

Remember establishments which have lax security become known to criminals and other undesirable people, whether they be terrorists, drug pushers, habitual drunks or prostitutes, and the word gets passed around. This means more and more undesirables will try to use the premises for their own ends. Once legitimate customers get to know they will cease to come. And this is bad for business.

 REMEMBER

Never give a stranger a guest's room number. When dealing with personal and telephone callers establish their name and the name of the guest they wish to contact. Then let the guest know who wants him or her and give the guest the option of being unavailable. (See units 27 and 38.) One occasion when you might direct a visitor to a guest's room is after receiving explicit instructions from the guest and being sure of the identity of the caller: 'Mr Bingham is due to arrive at 7 p.m. Please send him to my room.'

 TO DO

Get a colleague to try and find out information from you about a certain guest staying in the hotel. It can be an imaginary customer and an imaginary hotel. The idea is that your colleague, up to no good, is trying to catch you out. Your objective is to protect the security of the guest and the hotel.

Alternatively

Arrange with your tutor's or supervisor's help to visit an establishment where the security procedures have to be rigorous, for example a large conference centre. Speak to some of the staff concerned. What do they regard as the main security threats and how do they counteract them? Does the design of the building, for example the number and location of exits, cause any special security problems?

Banking

The receptionist may be expected to deposit the money he or she has taken during the shift into the establishment's safe, to be taken to the bank later by a manager or by a security company.

- When totalling the day's takings find a secure office and lock yourself in, or make sure you are in the presence of a manager or the establishment's security officer.
- Carry money in security bags.

Taking cash to the bank

In a small establishment it is possible the receptionists will be asked to transport the money to the bank during bank opening hours or to deposit it in a night safe at the bank.

- Use a vehicle if possible and transfer the money to the vehicle out of sight.
- Never establish a pattern of going to the bank at a regular time, or taking the same route.
- If possible take a colleague with you to act as a look out.
- Do not try to act heroically if you are attacked. Instead:
  - co-operate with the attacker, but giving away as little information as possible
  - note details about the attacker's physical appearance, manner of speech, any vehicle used, and the direction in which the attacker escapes. Never attempt to follow
  - alert the police and management immediately
  - do not handle anything the attacker has touched to preserve finger prints.

Cash is the easiest form of money to steal, and exchange for goods later, because it is difficult to trace. Cash should be kept in a locked container at all times when not use, either a drawer, the till or the safe. Where large amounts of cash are being counted, say when banking at the end of the day, the door should be locked

Care of guests' property

Arriving and departing guests make good targets for thieves and terrorists because luggage and other personal property is often left unattended.

- Check guests in and out as fast as possible so that luggage is left in reception for the least amount of time.
- Keep a wary eye out for anyone acting suspiciously.
- Always treat suitcases and other containers with care as they may burst or tear if handled roughly (see unit 37).
- Ask departing guests whether they have all their belongings with them: 'There, Mr Holmes (an absent minded guest), that seems to be all your luggage – shall I have a final check in your room?' Avoid appearing to be accusing or interrogating the guest.

Many establishments have a luggage room where guests can leave their cases. This should be kept securely locked when not in use and guests should be given a receipt for items deposited (see unit 23). This provides proof of ownership when the guest calls to collect the property (a different person may be on duty, or you may not remember what belongs to whom).

Remember to look after your own belongings as well as those of the customers. Keep your bag, purse and other valuables with you at all times. If you have a locker at work, use it

Lost property

Any member of staff discovering personal belongings which appear to have been left behind or mislaid by a customer, should hand them immediately to the person in charge of lost property.

- Note where and when the item(s) was found and by whom.
- Look for and note any clues to the owner, and get the help of anyone in the area at the time the property was discovered.
- When a claim is made for lost property ask for a description of the item. If there is any doubt that the claim is genuine, or the lost property is a particularly valuable item, ask a manager to deal with the matter.

Looking after guests' valuables

Most larger establishments have safe deposit boxes where guests can leave their valuables (see unit 23 and, for the legal aspects, unit 49). Alternatively guests may leave their valuables in the establishment's safe.

- Ask the guests to sign that the property has been left for safe-keeping, and issue a receipt.
- Each time the guest takes the property out of safe-keeping, he or she should be asked to sign and date the safe deposit record book. Check the signature is the same.
- If the valuables are kept in a sealed envelope, each time the seal is broken or the article removed you should ask the guest to replace it in another sealed container before accepting it for safe keeping.

Articles, such as fur coats, which are too large to fit in a safe, should be locked in a secure place.

When the guest checks out he or she should be politely asked to clear the box or safe (unless safe-keeping facilities are offered to non-resident guests), and a signature obtained to the effect that the box is now clear and the key has been returned.

The master key system means that the privacy of residents and guests is protected. Anyone not wishing to be disturbed by housekeeping or floor service staff can double lock the door from the inside. The grand master can be used in an emergency

 TO DO

Study this procedure for dealing with a suspicious-looking item and design a poster to explain the steps.
1. If you see a suspicious-looking item which might be a bomb, do not touch it yourself or let customers or colleagues put themselves in possible danger.
2. Raise the alarm.
3. Call for help, from the emergency services, and from management and security officers.
4. Help evacuate the building.

?? **HOW TO**

Deal with a bomb threat
1. Keep the person making the threat talking as long as possible. It will help if you can keep your voice calm and controlled.
2. While you are talking try and alert a colleague to what is going on. A telephone call can be traced if the authorities are alerted quickly and the conversation can be kept going.
3. Ask for the message/threat to be repeated, try to record the exact words and write them down as soon as possible.
4. Obtain as much information as you can about the whereabouts of the bomb.
5. Warn the person that the building is occupied and that the bomb could result in many deaths. If there are children, elderly, handicapped or sick people on the premises, or anyone else who is specially vulnerable, tell the person.
6. Listen carefully to the voice and to any background noises. Details on the accent of the caller, the sex, emotional state (calm, nervous, angry), the distant sounds of a train, busy road, people talking and laughing, can all help the police track down the person or organisation responsible.
7. If a colleague has not already been able to inform the police and management, do so yourself immediately.
8. Follow the emergency procedures laid down in your establishment.

In the event of an emergency such as fire the receptionist is usually responsible for phoning 999. Some receptions have direct links with the fire and other emergency services. It is important that front office staff are well-rehearsed in what they have to do, so that if a fire does break out they can act quickly and calmly. Staff are responsible not only for their own safety, but also that of the customers who are not usually so familiar with the layout of the building. By acting promptly and correctly the receptionist can save lives.

How fire starts

A fire results when there is a combination of fuel, heat and air.

Fuel This may be paper, wood, cooking oils, fabric or any other flammable material.

Heat This may originate from faulty electrical equipment or a cigarette end.

Air Air contains oxygen which enables the fire to burn.

How fire spreads

Open doors and windows will encourage fire to burn faster by increasing the supply of oxygen and fanning the flames. So close windows and doors if possible as soon as a fire breaks out.

As fire develops, smoke and gases, many of them poisonous, are produced. These are lighter than air and rise up until they encounter an obstacle such as a ceiling, where they spread out and pass horizontally through any opening into corridors, and from one storey to the next. Open doors, staircases and lift shafts all encourage the passage of smoke and gases.

Know what you have to do

Several members of staff will have specific tasks to carry out in the event of a fire. For instance knocking on bedroom doors to tell guests to leave the building. The receptionist is often responsible for taking the residents' list, departure list, and staff in and out book (if there is one) so that a count can be taken and missing people identified. The receptionist may also be required to take the cash box and room keys. The procedure will vary from establishment to establishment. The important thing is that the receptionist should know exactly what his or her tasks are.

The various types of extinguisher use a colour coding so they are easily recognisable. British Standard 5423 recommends that all extinguishers should be red with an additional colour code to indicate the extinguishing medium.

water – red   *carbon dioxide* – black
foam – cream   *halon* – green
dry powder – blue

Many extinguishers are still in use where the appropriate colour is the predominant colour – the whole cylinder is black or green, for example.

?? HOW TO

Take action in the event of a fire

If you discover a fire first
1. Remain calm.
2. Walk, don't run.
3. Raise the alarm by operating the nearest fire alarm.
4. Call for help using the procedure laid down by the establishment.
5. Attack the fire with the equipment provided but only if this will not put you in personal danger.
6. Leave the building with the guest by the nearest safe route and exit, giving help to those who need it. But do not risk your own life.

If you hear the fire alarm
1. Remain calm.
2. Walk, don't run.
3. Someone will be responsible for informing the switchboard or reception about the fire. Larger establishments have a direct emergency line to the switchboard and sometimes to the fire brigade, which staff should be aware of. Reception, switchboard or a manager in charge at the time will then call the fire brigade by dialling 999.
4. Rouse the guests and make sure they know there is a fire.
5. Leave the premises with the guests by the nearest safe route and exit, giving special help to those in need. But do not risk your own life in doing so.
6. Report to the person in charge at the assembly point outside.

Before leaving the building
The following precautions should be taken only if they do not endanger life. It is important to remain calm when making these split-second decisions.
1. Switch off all electrical and gas appliances.
2. Close all windows and doors which will not be used during the evacuation.
3. Close doors after everyone has passed through.
4. Only collect handbags and other valuable or important personal possessions if these are nearby. Never attempt to collect belongings from elsewhere in the building. Guests must be dissuaded from going to their rooms to fetch valuables.

At the assembly point
Once at the assembly point remain there until told by a person in authority that it is safe to leave.
- Never return to the building to collect something.
- Do not return to the building to check for missing people. Inform the fire officer or someone in authority.

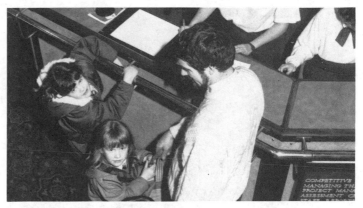

Guests, customers, and other people who do not work on the premises, are particularly vulnerable when a fire breaks out:
- *they are in surroundings they do not know*
- *they may not have read the fire instructions in their room*
- *they may not understand the language*
- *in hospitals, the residents are generally infirm and will need extra help*
- *in residential establishments they may be elderly, very young or disabled and will need special help*

Do not let yourself or your colleagues get into lax habits at work. Staff have a legal responsibility to report any fire, health or safety hazards including dangerous working practices even if this means telling on your colleagues, or them on you

Most receptionists' jobs require the ability to type because there is usually a fair amount of administration to be done, for instance records, guest lists, menus and communications to other departments. Typing is done on the keyboard (a display of letters of the alphabet and other functions) of a typewriter, word processor or other computer, or a telex (see unit 29).

!! **REMEMBER**

Regularly back up or copy on a floppy disc all information contained on a computer. Then if there is loss or distortion to the data held on the computer, the back-up copies can be used (once the problem has been corrected) to restore the situation to what it was when the back up was made. The work carried out since the last back up will be lost but this should be at the most one day's work.

A word processor can automatically: delete mistakes, print out page after page, print out hundreds of address labels for envelopes, print out several copies of the same letter, but addressed to individuals by name

Keyboards

All keyboards are similar, no matter what kind of equipment is being used, in that they have a key for each letter of the alphabet. When this is pressed the corresponding letter is typed on the paper or is shown on the visual display (monitor). Where the keyboard of, say, a word processor and a typewriter may differ is in the so-called function keys. These are keys which tell the machine to change lines, indent a paragraph, roll down the page, and so on. Word processors require many more function keys than do most typewriters because they are programmed to do various typing tasks automatically. Each key tells the machine what to do.

Although keyboards of telex, computers and word processors may look daunting at first, there is a logic to using them which, once mastered, can make these machines a joy to use. Especially if you are used to an old manual typewriter!

The parts of a computer

Central processing unit (CPU) The CPU processes information and makes calculations, but unlike the human brain it is not capable of independent thought. The CPU can operate only according to pre-set instructions. It scans information and processes it according to set rules.

Input unit This feeds in information and relays instructions to the computer. The input unit is often a keyboard (much like the keyboard of a typewriter). Information can also be loaded into the computer from a cassette or floppy disc, via cables or the telephone line from another computer, by using a magnetic or optical character reader and, in the case of the very large computers, from magnetic tape and punched cards. Most microcomputers can be instructed what to do next by using a hand-held control called a mouse, or with some models, by touching the screen in a certain place.

Memory unit Information is stored in the memory. A part of the memory provides facilities always needed by the computer. It is permanently stored and cannot be altered hence its name Read Only Memory or ROM. Another part of the memory, RAM or Random Access Memory, stores information that can be altered, read and replaced with other information. Data in the RAM area is normally lost when the computer is switched off. Once the computer has carried out an operation the result can be stored in a back-up memory unit until it is ready to be used or needs amending. When required the CPU transmits data from the memory to the output unit.

Output unit This passes information to the user – words or pictures displayed on a screen (also called a *monitor* or *visual display unit* or *VDU*), or printed on to a sheet of paper. It can also transfer the information on to a disc or magnetic tape for storage and future processing, perhaps by another computer. There may be a direct link to another computer by telephone line, for example.

USEFUL TERMS

Hardware The parts of the computer that you can touch and are permanent or not easily changed, for example the keyboard, screen and the printer.

Software The instructions, or programs, that tell the hardware what to do.

Program A set of instructions to the computer on what to do with the information fed into it. Every piece of data fed into a (digital) computer is changed into the digit 0 or the digit 1. Since it is not really convenient to communicate with a computer using just 0 or 1 various programming languages have been developed to get around the problem. One example is BASIC, which stands for Beginners' All-purpose Symbolic Instruction Code.

Word processing The writing, editing, storing and sorting of text using computer technology instead of pen and paper or a typewriter.

Disc storage system Where computer programs and information are held.

Hard copy Information printed by a printer attached to the computer.

TO DO

Try to persuade someone to give you a lesson on how to write a short letter on a word processor. Write down step by step what you have to do and the purpose of the different function keys you need to use.

The keyboard of this energy control monitor is not like that on a word processor. From reception the temperature of each room in the hotel can be adjusted individually. This helps reduce energy costs and provides a comfortable environment suited to the needs of each guest

Touch typing

Maybe you have watched in awe at the speed at which some typists can work at the keyboard. It is a matter of practice, but also of learning the right way from the start. Touch typing is a method by which all the fingers of both hands are used and the typist has learnt by heart the location and function of all the main keys, so she or he is able to work without looking at the keyboard. This can be particularly useful when copy typing (say copying a hand written letter) because the typist can keep his or her eye on the written letter the whole time without having to stop to look at the keyboard and then back at the letter.

There are courses in touch typing. Some are very expensive. You may be lucky enough to find that your local library has a cassette tape, and all you will then need is to borrow a typewriter. Alternatively you can borrow a library book on how to touch type, and make yourself a card or paper keyboard. Once you know which fingers are used for which keys, it is just a matter of practice and more practice.

The fastest typists can type 60 words a minute and more. Compare this with the rate at which you can write by hand. However most employers will be satisfied with speeds of 30 to 45 words a minute for receptionists

Information is stored so that it can be retrieved when required. For instance you may want to search through the guest history card of a certain Mr Longsbury who is due to arrive the next day. You remember he had very strong preferences about a number of things during his previous stay and you want to check exactly what these were to help you provide the kind of service he requires. If your filing system is logical and easy to use you would probably find Mr Longsbury's card filed alphabetically under L.

An effective filing system is essential if you and other people are going to be able to find the information needed quickly and easily. This means:

- storing the right information (which will be required)
- using a logical system of classifying information which can be understood by other people
- storing information for the right length of time (too long is a waste of space and therefore not cost effective)
- making sure the information is adequately protected (will not be deleted on the computer or thrown away from the filing cabinet).

TO DO

Find out what methods of storing information are used in your place of work or college department office, and in two further hotel, catering, leisure and tourism establishments of your choice. Write a short report describing the systems used, their advantages and disadvantages.

On the basis of your investigation what system would you recommend to a friend who has just taken over a medium sized hotel. The hotel is located on the outskirts of a large city, close to the international airport and the motorway.

Classifying information

Chronological order By the date. This method is ideal for reservations correspondence. For example a separate file is kept for each day of the month for the next 12 months, for each month in the following year, and for each year after that. A decision is made on when the month and year files are likely to get so full it is difficult to find information. These files will then be sub-divided into the shorter time period.

The correspondence is filed under the date of arrival, possibly in alphabetic order. A disadvantage of this system is that you have to know the exact date before information can be retrieved. When reservations are changed from one date to another it is best to leave a note in the first file indicating where the correspondence has been moved to (see unit 31).

Alphabetical order Organised in the same order as the letters of the alphabet. This method is easy to understand and new records can be easily added. There may be some confusion about where to file 'Mackintosh' and 'McIntosh', or a company called 'GCE Electric Wholesalers' or 'House of Alabaster', and will the information be under 'Transmarche Tunnel Diggers' or 'TTD', and if it is 'TTD' is the proper place at the beginning of the T section, or towards the end, after 'Tsavolitch'? If guidelines are decided in advance these difficulties should not arise. With the high standards of accuracy that are required in front office operations another typical difficulty of this system should not arise: uncertainty about how to spell a person's name, for example is it 'Lines' or 'Lynes'?

Filing cabinets like the one below (which use the so-called vertical system) require a certain amount of space because the drawer has to be opened to gain access to the files. Another system (known as the lateral system) uses cupboards, with the files hanging in rows from runners. The file identification is on the outer edge. The lower photograph shows a concertina box file divided into a section for each letter of the alphabet. The open box contains the reservations relating to the 20th of the current month, filed in alphabetic order

Geographical order Filed by country and/or region. This method is useful in a sales office where contacts are maintained with the travel trade in various overseas countries, or there are regular dealings with regional and area tourist boards, or branches of the Rotary Club. If the correspondence relating to Australia for example becomes large that particular file can be sub-divided into alphabetical order.

Subject order This method brings together all the documents relating to insurance, training, stationery suppliers or hirers of audio visual equipment. It is convenient and allows for unlimited expansion but it is difficult to know where to put miscellaneous information. Files which become too large can be split up into alphabetical order by company name.

An alternative is to combine subject and numeric order. For example under 'Suppliers': '1. Letterhead', '2. Envelopes', '3. Printer ribbons'. With this system new categories can be added without re-arranging the order of all existing files. For instance when a new laser printer is acquired for producing guest bills, a category '4. Laser printer supplies' is added to the filing system.

Numerical order An accurate system which can be easily expanded, particularly if there are sub-divisions such as 6.3, 6.4, 6.4.1, 6.4.2 and so forth. It is ideal for paid guest bills, order forms and other documents that have a serial number printed or stamped on them. Sometimes such documents are filed in numerical order by date, for example paid guest bills relating to 15 March 1992.

This rotary filing system is used to store the registration cards which have been prepared for the day's arrivals. There is a divider card corresponding to each room number. One side of the carousel is in the reception area, the other side in the reservations office, so staff from either department can gain immediate access

---

 GUESTCRAFT TIPS

- If a file is needed and will be away from its normal storage place for some time a note or marker should be left of its whereabouts. Colleagues will not waste energy searching for it.
- If a document could be filed under two or more different headings, cross-reference it to remind everyone where it has been placed. Under each of the alternative headings place a note referring to the actual location.

The card index system on the right of this computer is a favourite way for organising guest history cards, reservation details and so forth. Nowadays computers play an important role in storing information, much of which can be automatically transferred from one area to another – for example from the reservations record to the guest history card. Files can take up a great deal of space. Imagine the registration cards of a 800 bedroom hotel where the average stay is one day (the cards must be kept for at least 12 months by law). A solution is to microfilm the cards: record the details in miniaturised form on a strip of film. A special machine is used to read the film – you will see one in most large libraries

When the receptionist sends letters and parcels to customers and business companies, there is usually one method of dispatch which is more appropriate than any of the others. Factors which may influence the choice include: cost, distance, time, size of package, destination (town or country, inland or overseas), type of customer or business.

First class mail   For letters and small packages which contain important information that should be received quickly. The Post Office aims to deliver first class mail the day after collection, and recommended posting times (in some cases early in the afternoon) are based on this. The basic charge covers items weighing up to 60 g, with a sliding scale that increases the costs substantially for heavier items.

Second class mail   This service is cheaper than first class mail but delivery will take three or more days depending on the handling and distance involved. The upper weight limit means that small packages over 750 g have to be sent by another method. The basic charge covers items weighing up to 60 g.

Bulk mail discounts   When large numbers of letters are going to be sent at the same time the Post Office will give the sender a discount of around 10%. Certain conditions are laid down including the use of a post code for each address.

Business reply service   A company with a business reply licence can supply its customers with a special envelope or postcard (the design and size of which have to be approved by the Post Office) to make correspondence with that company easier (no need to address the envelope) and free (the postage is paid by the company). The Post Office charges the company for the number of business reply letters delivered at the appropriate postage rate (the service can be used for first or second class mail) plus a small surcharge.

Freepost   Licenced companies can give their customers a special freepost address (which may be rather shorter than the normal address and usually has a different post code), for example:

   Grand Hotel, FREEPOST, Piddleton-on-Sea PD5 6BR

Customers can use their own envelopes, or the company can provide pre-printed envelopes (in which case freepost has no advantage on the reply paid service). Freepost mail is handled as second class mail and the recipient pays the appropriate postage plus a surcharge.

Certificate of posting   A free service for ordinary classes of mail, but issued on request only. (A compensation claim for lost mail should be supported by evidence of posting if it is to have any chance of succeeding.)

Special delivery   This is for next working day delivery even if the item arrives at its destination sorting office too late for the normal delivery of the day. A certificate of posting records the time the package is accepted and the signature of the addressee is obtained on delivery.

  TO DO

Over the next few occasions when the post is sent from an establishment you are familiar with, identify five items that need to be sent by a service other than first class or second class mail. Explain the service you would choose for each item and your reasons. Check your choices with the person responsible for handling the mail and with that person's help establish the cost and what special Post Office procedures would have to be followed.

Price is usually an important factor when deciding how to send a letter or parcel. Always find out how much it will cost before committing yourself

Private courier companies provide an express delivery service, particularly across towns and cities. They can be expensive because your item is usually transported individually, often by motorbike. An alternative is to send the item by British Rail's Red Star service. The package can be taken to the Red Star office at the local railway station by the sender and collected by the addressee from his or her nearest railway station. For extra fees Red Star will arrange collection and delivery by courier. Urgent items can also be sent by fax (see unit 14) or from one computer terminal to another (*electronic mail*).

Datapost This is a more expensive service than special delivery, but next working day delivery (by 10 a.m. for two-thirds of the UK) is guaranteed (or compensation will be paid). This service is also available for urgent overseas mail. Proof of posting and of delivery are provided.

Recorded delivery A service for first and second class mail which provides proof of posting and of delivery in return for an extra fee. No compensation is payable for money or articles of value sent by this service.

Registered mail This service (available for first class mail only) provides proof of posting and delivery and special security handling. Three levels of compensation are available (but never higher than the value of the lost goods) and consequential loss insurance for items which are worth more than their material value (for example a computer disc containing important data). There are restrictions on the way in which registered packages can be sealed. All joins in the packaging must be glued or fixed with sealing tape and the seal has to be signed across so that it will be immediately apparent if the package has been tampered with. String is not permissible. For currency or other forms of monetary worth the special registered letter envelope must be used.

Airmail, Swiftair and airparcel For sending letters and packages to overseas countries outside Europe using international and national airlines (with Swiftair providing accelerated treatment in the UK and express delivery abroad where this is available) as opposed to *surface mail* when the items are sent by sea and overland transport for the entire journey. The weight bands are much narrower than inland mail, so the service is more cost effective when special lightweight airmail envelopes and paper are used. (All mail to Europe is sent by air wherever possible at the same cost as a first class letter in the UK.)

Parcel post services Normal parcel post is the most economical Post Office service for heavier items but relatively slow. *Compensation fee parcel post* provides a certificate of posting and higher compensation for loss or damage. Overseas parcels can be sent surface mail or airmail depending on their urgency. For many countries the extra cost for airmail is not significantly higher than surface mail (itself quite expensive). Insurance is available on overseas parcels. Express delivery ensures the parcels get the earliest possible delivery when they arrive in the destination country. Customs clearance abroad can be speeded up by using the *Franc de Droits* service: the sender pre-pays customs and other charges that would otherwise have to be paid by the addressee.

Printed paper post This reduces the cost of airmailing printed material such as brochures to overseas customers. It must be easy for the authorities to check the contents (see unit 17). There is a strict limit on the number of handwritten words so Christmas cards with a few words of greeting can be sent airmail printed paper provided they are not sealed. Printed paper can also be sent surface mail under similar conditions. The package should state 'Printed paper reduced rate'.

Intelpost Documents are sent by fax (provided the sending and receiving Post Offices have a fax machine).

Poste Restante Items are kept at the specified Post Office until collected by the addressee. This is useful when someone travelling abroad cannot give a forwarding address.

Telemessages and telegrams Within the UK urgent messages can be sent to a person not on the telephone by the British Telecom telemessage service. Telegrams to overseas countries are also sent via British Telecom (see unit 59).

Franking machines

These avoid the need to stick stamps on individual envelopes. The postage rate is selected by the operator and then the machine will print the value paid, the date of posting, the company's licence number (under which it is authorised to use a franking machine) and possibly a short advertising message and/or the company's logo on the envelope. When envelopes and packages are too bulky to go through the franking machine a special label is used which can be stuck on to the package.

Mail which has been franked is normally handed over a Post Office counter, or bagged and collected from the company by arrangement with the Post Office. It should not be mixed up with ordinary mail, so if it has to be put in a letter box a special envelope provided by the Post Office must be used.

The franking machine is taken to the Post Office from time to time to be credited with units. These are paid for in advance and allow the user to frank mail to a value of say £500.

 GUESTCRAFT TIP

If a company is too small to have its own franking machine but wants to mail a large number of letters for a particular reason (a direct mail campaign for example) these can be left with the Post Office for franking. The postage is pre-paid on the basis of the number, weight and destination of the letters.

ADC call One way of finding out how long a particular call has lasted and how much it has cost to make, is to place the call via the British Telecom operator, stating that you wish to make an ADC call and giving the number you require and your own number. After the call has been completed the operator will call you back and 'advise the duration and cost' (hence the name of the service).

Fixed time call This service is available via the international operator. It is mostly used when the telephone lines to a particular country are often engaged, or if you know the person who needs to take the call will be available at a certain time. At Christmas and other busy times several days' advance warning may be required for a fixed time call.

Reverse charge call Also known as a collect call this service is used when the person being called is asked to pay for the cost of the call. The British Telecom operator will give the name of the person calling and ask if a reverse charge call can be accepted.

Person to person call This type of call is used when the caller wishes to speak to a particular person, for example in large company in Delhi, India. It is more expensive than a normal call placed through the operator, but if the person is unavailable no charge is incurred.

Telemessages and telegrams A quick way of contacting people who live in the UK but do not have a telephone is through British Telecom's telemessage service. The message given to the BT operator is telexed through to the nearest connection and delivered by special delivery.

Telegrams can still be sent to overseas countries. The message is taken by the BT operator who deals with overseas telegrams, then telexed to the destination country. Once there it will be delivered by special messenger or in many countries phoned through and a confirmation copy sent in the normal post.

Freefone and local rate calls Freefone is the British Telecom equivalent of freepost (see unit 51). The cost of a call made to any number beginning with 0800 is paid by the subscriber.

A freefone call can also be made via the British Telecom operator by dialling 100. Ask to be connected with the freefone name or number you require. The name is usually a catchy one such as Enterprise (used by the Small Firms Service).

If you call a number beginning with 0345 the call will be charged at local rates, no matter where you are calling in the UK. The subscriber pays the additional cost.

Information services A variety of information services are operated by British Telecom from the speaking clock which gives an accurate time setting to recorded messages on the weather, the latest Test Match score and gardening tips.

Alarm calls The British Telecom operator will call a specified number at the

Shown in this photograph is a PABX telephone switchboard (see unit 14). The desktop control is quite small and neat. The bulkier back-up equipment is out of sight in a cupboard

---

◆ ◆ ◆ **TO DO**

Obtain an up-to-date copy of British Telecom's *Guide to telephone charges* (available free by telephoning your local BT district offices during normal working hours). Then calculate the cost of making a six minute international call to a country of your choice:
- via the international operator
- dialled direct in the cheap, standard and, if available, peak period.

Then based on the three or four price comparisons you have worked out prepare a short information sheet which could be used to explain the options to trainee front office staff.

time and on the day required. Usually the hotel's own staff (telephone operator or receptionist) will make alarm calls to guest rooms free, but for other types of residential establishment and for small hotels the BT service is a valuable standby.

Credit card calls British Telecom will issue credit cards to subscribers who often make calls from a phone other than their own. The cost of these calls can then be charged direct to the subscriber saving any embarrassment or difficulty in settling costs with the people kind enough to lend their phone.

Some payphones accept standard credit cards, such as Barclaycard and Access, as an alternative to paying in large quantities of coins or buying a phonecard.

❊ FOR INTEREST

Prestel is a viewdata service offered by British Telecom. Using an adapted television set, a hand-held monitor and a telephone line the user has access to many pages of information held in the system. From the main menu the user selects what sort of information he or she requires, for instance hotels. A further choice, say of hotels in various cities, is then offered. Quite quickly the user can obtain information on a specific hotel and if it is suitable make a booking by answering the questions which appear on the screen. Holiday brochures can be requested in the same way and goods purchased from suppliers.

Ceefax (operated by the BBC) and Oracle (operated by Independent Television) are two teletext services using the normal television signal. Pages of text can be viewed on the user's television set (provided it is equipped with a decoder) and by making various selections more detailed information can be found about the latest cricket Test Match results or the weather.

This telephone exchange system is linked to a computer which logs the details of all numbers called (guests can dial any number in the world direct from their room) including the charge the hotel will make the caller. (This is somewhat higher than the charge made by British Telecom in order to recoup the cost of the equipment and contribute to the employment costs of the telephone operators.) If the equipment goes wrong the operators put a bar on all but local calls. Anyone wishing to make a long distance call then has to ask the hotel operator to get the number. The hotel operator asks the British Telecom operator to connect the number as an ADC call. This is the only way the cost of phone calls can be kept track of and properly charged to guests during an equipment malfunction – fortunately a rare occurrence

---

❢❢ REMEMBER

- The sooner an out of order telephone line is reported the quicker it can be repaired by the British Telecom engineers. Valuable business may be lost if customers are unable to contact the establishment.
- The least expensive time for making telephone calls within the UK is at weekends, or between 6 p.m. and 8 a.m. on Mondays to Fridays. Calls made on weekdays between 8 a.m. and 9 a.m. and between 1 p.m. and 6 p.m. are cheaper than calls made between 9 a.m. and 1 p.m., the peak period.
- Distance also affects the cost of a call. Local calls are cheapest, calls to numbers less than about 56 km (about 35 miles) away fall in the next price band, calls to numbers in the UK which are further away than this come in a more expensive price band, while calls to mobile phones are charged at the highest rate of all.
- It costs more to make an international call via the operator than it does to dial it yourself, and many countries can now be dialled direct.
- The cost of an international call also varies according to the time of day (and this will depend on what time it is in the country you are calling), the length of the call and the charge band for the country concerned.
- The minimum charge for a call placed via the operator is for a three minute call.

Credit cards

Credit card companies issue cards to people who they believe are credit worthy. Charges are made to the card by the customer up to a pre-set limit which will vary from customer to customer. The amount outstanding on the card (the balance) has to be paid each month, in full or in part, within a certain time of the statement being issued. The minimum repayment permitted is set by the government (under the Consumer Credit Act). Many card companies also require the customer to pay an annual fee for use of the card.

Some establishments accept payment by any of the principal credit cards, others will only accept one or perhaps two. Various factors influence the decision, for example:

- which credit cards the establishment's customers seem to be using or want to use
- what the particular credit card company charges the establishment for the service. Generally this will be a percentage of what customers have charged to the credit card and is deducted when the credit card company reimburses the establishment.

A maximum limit (sometimes called the floor limit) is imposed on what establishments can charge to a customer's credit card without obtaining authorisation from the credit card company that the customer has sufficient credit available. The amount usually depends on the size of the business; it may be £50 or rather higher, for example £150.

Establishments would be foolish not to go along with the trend when it comes to which credit cards customers like to use. Make sure you inform management if you notice a significant number of customers presenting a credit card which your company does not accept

 FOR INTEREST

The major credit card companies include American Express, Diners Club and Carte Blanche, and the various banks which operate Visa and Mastercard. For example the Barclays Bank version of Visa is Barclaycard, and the Royal Bank of Scotland is one of the banks who use Access.

Trusthouse Forte, Holiday Inns and Swallow Hotels are examples of large hotel and catering companies which issue their own credit cards (just as many retailers do, for instance the John Lewis Partnership, Marks and Spencer and House of Fraser). The service appeals to regular customers, particularly if it entitles them to superior accommodation, a discount or other special privileges. It also has advantages for the company, encouraging customer loyalty, providing extra income (from service fees and interest charges on outstanding accounts) and avoiding the commission which would have to be paid if the customer used a Visa card, for example.

Some hotel, catering, leisure and tourism establishments have a direct computer link with the credit card company which displays the authorisation code or action to be taken on a screen or printout. This speeds up the process of authorisation and is more discreet than telephoning (see units 20 and 46).

Some credit card companies issue gold cards which do not have a set credit limit for the cardholder. If the charge is above the establishment's floor limit for that type of card the credit card company's authorisation is still required before the charge can be accepted.

Barclaycard (Visa) credit cards can also be used as a cheque guarantee card (see unit 45). Sometimes the card is purely a cheque card (if the cardholder does not have a Barclaycard account).

Direct debit cards such as Switch and Connect look like credit or cheque guarantee cards. They also have to be imprinted like a credit card and the voucher signed by the customer. The difference is that the money is withdrawn directly from the customer's current bank account, like a cheque. Provided the customer has sufficient funds in his or her account and the accepting establishment gets authorisation, there is no limit to the amount which can be charged to a direct debit card account, unlike a cheque.

Bank cheques

Cheques which are *crossed* may only be paid into a bank account and may not be cashed. Generally cheques are crossed at the same time they are over-printed with the account number and name and various bank details. But a customer can request an *open* cheque book or *uncross* a cheque by writing 'Pay cash' between the lines.

A crossed cheque can be *endorsed*, in other words made payable to a different account holder. The name of the new payee is written on the back of the cheque by the original payee and signed by the authorised signatory. This process can be repeated.

If a cheque has *A/c payee* written or printed between the crossing it may only be paid into the account of the person, organisation or company to whom the cheque was originally made out.

Banks will return a cheque which is over six months old to the payee un-paid. The payee is responsible for contacting the person who originally made out the *stale* cheque and resolving the situation (which may be a quite inno-cent mistake, for example the payee has written 3 January 1990, when it should be 1991, or the result of the cheque being mislaid for a rather long time).

Banks will also return a cheque which has not been supported by a cheque guarantee card (see unit 45) when there are insufficient funds in the payee's account. The cheque will state *refer to drawer* and the establishment must then contact the payee to obtain payment in some other way.

The payee can *stop* a cheque provided it has not already been cleared through the banking system nor guaranteed by a cheque card. This might happen when the payee decides not to honour the payment, and perhaps plans to return the goods or to pay in some other way. Alternatively the payee may suspect that the cheque has been lost.

USEFUL TERMS

Standing order Instructions to the bank to pay a certain amount of money at a specified and usually regular interval to a particular account. For example rather than face one large business rates bill each year, the amount can be paid in ten monthly instalments. Standing orders can run for a specified period, as in the rates example, or indefinitely.

Direct debit Instructions to the bank to pay to a particular account whatever sum of money is due at specified intervals. For example community charges can be paid to local authorities by direct debit. The person concerned chooses from various instalment options, for instance two payments at an interval of six months, four quarterly payments or ten monthly payments. Once a year all the local authority has to do is advise the account holder and the bank on the amount of each payment. Unlike standing orders, direct debits do not have to be amended by the account holder each time the amount of money changes.

 TO DO

You want to open up a new current account, or give advice to a friend in this situation. To help you make your decision find out the various services and facilities offered by the banks and building societies convenient for where you (or your friend) live and work. Information can be obtained by visiting the premises and asking at the enquiry desk, by collecting and studying brochures displayed on the premises, or from the personal finance columns of newpapers and magazines. Your queries may cover:

- bank charges and how these are levied
- how interest can be earned
- cheque guarantee cards
- cash withdrawal cards and which cash machines they can be used with
- direct debit cards
- overdraft facilities and charges
- any free gift offers
- credit card facilities and charges
- standing order/direct debit facilities
- number of branches
- supporting services offered (mortgages, home loans, insurance and so forth).

Alternatively

Find out what countries use the following currency. In some cases the list is very long, so a selection will do.

dollar/cents	Deutsche Mark/pfennigs	dinar/fils
drachma/lepta	escudo/centavos	franc/centimes
guilder/cents	krona/öre	krone/øre
lira/piastres	yen/sen	peseta/céntimos

When accepting payment by credit card or cheque be sure to follow the procedures to prevent fraud, see units 45 and 46

INDEX

INDEX